Images of Family Life in Magazine Advertising: 1920-1978

Images of Family Life in Magazine Advertising: 1920-1978

by Bruce W. Brown

PRAEGER STUDIES ON CHANGING ISSUES IN THE FAMILY

General Editor
Suzanne K. Steinmetz

PRAEGER SPECIAL STUDIES • PRAEGER SCIENTIFIC

Brown, Bruce W.
    Images of family life in magazine advertising, 1920–1978.

    (Praeger studies on changing issues in the family)
    Bibliography: p.
    Includes indexes.
    1. Family—United States—History—20th century.
2. Advertising, Magazine—Social aspects—United States.
3. Sex role in advertising—United States—History—20th century.
I. Title. II. Series.
HQ536.B773   306.8'0973   81–14366
ISBN 0–03–059697–1   AACR2

Published in 1981 by Praeger Publishers
CBS Educational and Professional Publishing
A Division of CBS, Inc.
521 Fifth Avenue, New York, New York 10175 U.S.A.

© 1981 by Praeger Publishers

123456789   145   987654321

Printed in the United States of America

To Anna and Jason. Thanks for waiting.

Acknowledgments

Special thanks to the following: To Sieglinde Fizz and Ann Moore for typing the final drafts in spite of my perfectionism; to Saundra Gardner Atwell for our discussions on visual sociology during the early conception of this study; to Pamela Rosenberg for her assistance with the computer analysis; to John Natzke for his encouragement and support; to Suzanne Steinmetz, Darret Rutman, Fred Samuels, and Larry Hansen for their critiques of earlier drafts; to Murray Straus, who—although I accept all responsibility for any deficiencies in this book—has taught me how to research and write.

Finally, to Anna, my wife and research assistant, for her encouragement and support, for coauthoring the second chapter, and for making the entire book immeasurably more readable through her editing.

Wilkes College
Wilkes-Barre, Pennsylvania
June, 1981

B.W.B.

Foreword

There is probably no other area more in the public focus than that of the family. The decade of the 1970s can probably be labeled the decade of family awareness, culminating in the 1980 White House Conference on the Family. The 1980s also ushered in a pro-family, conservative President and the election of federal, state, and local officials whose platform often emphasized a stand on prayers in schools, busing, and abortion.

However, while research is continually measuring our current attitudes and behaviors on a wide variety of topics, it is also important to take the time to reflect on our attitudes toward the family in the past. Bruce Brown's book, *Images of Family Life in Magazine Advertising*, provides a mechanism to analyze changes in family roles, companionship, and intimacy as reflected in magazine advertisements. The book focuses on the images of the family over times, (the years between 1920 and 1978) as well as over the family life cycle (married with no children to postparental stages).

One of Brown's major goals is to overcome the lack of adequate longitudinal designs on which to compare the family. The increasing divorce rate, illegitimacy rates, family instability, and inadequate care of the elderly are often portrayed as contemporary problems with no historical background. Thus, by using advertisements from magazines that reach the working/middle class general readership we can assess the types of images that advertisers felt would be most appealing to this segment of the population.

Brown clearly warns us not to interpret these advertisements as indicators of the actual way that people behaved or the attitudes that they shared, but rather to indicate the behaviors and attitudes considered to be socially desirable. A comparison of the advertisements with available research and census data indicates the firmness with which these socially desirable images and beliefs are held.

For example, in an era when a large number of women were seeking work, woman's major role was still being portrayed as homemaker in ads. Nonetheless, this tells us something about what was valued even if it was not possible for all individuals to attain these goals. Thus, advertisements as a reflection of family life values are useful because they reflect cultural values concerning family life, as well as reflecting them as the idealized life families hope to obtain. They are not subjected to distortion or recollection, which becomes a problem in doing post-hoc research.

Brown's study utilized 521 randomly selected advertisements depicting family life, which appeared in general reader magazines between the years 1920 and 1977. The changes in the relationship between stages in the life cycles and family interaction over time were investigated. Major trends were not surprising. Women were rarely shown in occupational roles, and when they were featured in these roles it was doing work in the home to supplement family income. Furthermore, women were not shown in this role while young children were present, a direct contradiction to demographic data. Another finding that differs from demographic data was the strong emphasis on child care during the year of 1931 at a time when the birth rate was at its lowest. From a high point in 1931 this emphasis consistently decreased, even through the years of the baby boom. Apparently the need to reinforce our stereotyped view of ideal family remains constant in spite of data to the contrary.

Likewise, these trends seem to closely follow the employment patterns. For example, there is a fairly consistent decrease in advertisements depicting wives involved in housework since 1920. This finding is consistent with research findings that housekeeping is declining as a major family role, although the hours spent in the housekeeping tasks have remained constant since 1920. The only departure from this trend was the increased use of women involved in housework found in advertisements between 1945 and 1960—the era known for being the post-World War II decade of the baby boom generation.

Perhaps, as Brown suggests, it is the lack of prestige attached to household roles that accounts for the decline in advertisements featuring women in housework roles. However, it is the younger wife, one with no children or preschool children, where the greatest decrease was found. It is possible that the older woman feels more comfortable in her more traditional role, while the younger women, expected to be "super mom," "sex bomb," "career woman" rolled into one, needs a variety of role models for reinforcement. A recent TV perfume commercial touts the advantages of their product while showing the dutiful homemaker in a bathrobe cooking up a meal; in a business suit, obviously the career woman; and finally in a sexy outfit, ready for her mate.

One does need to address the issue of the effect of marketing research on the development of these advertisements. Are the media moguls using research that suggests that women with young children will have less time to engage in complex leisure time activities (such as sophisticated dinner parties or elaborate camping trips) and therefore not showing her in these somewhat unrealistic activities? Likewise, the couple in the preparental stage, or the family with much older children, might be more actively involved in these types of activities, and thus the recreational image is a realistic model to portray. Or is this an idealized view of families perpetrated by Madison Avenue with an attempt to mold families' behaviors, attitudes, and life styles to fit their product?

While the book provides interesting insights into family life in the past, perhaps its most provocative use will be as information for a starting point to an understanding of how ads might shape family life today.

In the 1960s an advertisement featuring a black woman was considered to be a liability unless the product being promoted was specifically for blacks, such as make-up or hair preparation. Advertisers felt that the white, middle-class individual would not relate to a black as a role model. Now almost every commercial, especially those featuring small children, looks like a UNICEF poster. Obviously, this has not hurt sales and may have increased our awareness and acceptance of minority groups. We need to ask: "Will Johnny be more accepting of Juana, Answar, Little Feather, and Zhimei in his classroom because he sees Spanish, middle Eastern, native American, and Oriental children playing with each other in a magazine advertisment?"

We also ask what subtle influence viewing these advertisements has on family life. For example, if we start showing the three- or four-child family, will the subtle message go out that three children or four children are the ideal. If we show the one-child family, especially if the child is preteen or teenage, which indicates that no other children are being planned, will this increase the desirability of the one-child family?

As a nation becoming more strongly divided on certain family-related decisions, the effect of these advertisements must not be minimized. Through the use of advertising reflecting the ideal family life behavior and attitudes, we can do much to shape the future family goals.

Suzanne K. Steinmetz
Series Editor

Table of Contents

List of Tables

List of Figures

ixx

List of Illustrations

Images of Family Life
in Magazine Advertising:
1920-1978

There is one traveler whose path the sociologist will cross more often than anyone else's on his journeys. This is the historian. The sociological journey will be much impoverished unless it is punctuated frequently by conversation with that other particular traveler.

Peter L. Berger

CHAPTER *I*

The Study of
Family Life

During the past 15 years the study of family roles[1] has taken on a new importance, partly due to the growth of the feminist movement. It now appears that as a society we are attempting to rectify some of the inequalities inherent in traditional family roles. The passage of the Equal Rights Amendment by a majority of the necessary 38 states, the emergence of a men's liberation movement, albeit in its embryonic stages, as well as the introduction and popularity of college courses dealing specifically with sex and family roles are among the trends toward this modification. These events suggest that there is a relatively high level of agreement that changes in family roles may be necessary.

Along with this emphasis on family roles, there has been much discussion within the general populace and among social scientists regarding "how the family used to be" and "how much the family has changed." We have, however, only recently begun to investigate such issues in an historical perspective. Gordon and Hareven (1973, p. 393) point out that the family of half a century ago or earlier has

---

[1] In the present study the terms "sex role" and "family role" will be used. Sex role is defined as "the expected behaviors attached to the differing social positions of male and female" (Scanzoni and Scanzoni 1976, p. 16). Family role refers to the expected behaviors attached to differing family positions such as mother, father, brother, sister, grandparent, etc.

1

been either ignored or romanticized. It is this author's contention that it is not only the family of half a century ago or earlier that has been ignored or romanticized, but that family sociologists in general have been *ahistorical* in their methods while *historical* in their conclusions; we revel in talking about change when, in fact, the historical evidence has been scanty at best.

CHANGES IN SEX AND FAMILY ROLES: PREVIOUS RESEARCH

Numerous studies have analyzed twentieth century changes in sex and family roles.[2] Although adding much to our knowledge, these studies, nevertheless, suffer from a number of deficiencies.

Lack of adequate longitudinal designs

The majority of the research has not been longitudinal, and those studies that are cover relatively short time periods. For example, in a 1975 study Parelius covers only a four-year span from 1969 to 1973. In her analysis of changes in college women's sex and family role attitudes, she found that such changes do not signal the end of marriage and motherhood, but rather that women are seeking a "restructuring of the family." Notions of equal responsibility for financial support, increased assistance with household tasks from husbands, and the importance of careers for married women were held by a substantial majority of women by 1973.

In a more extended analysis, Mason, Czajka, and Arber (1976), using public opinion surveys from 1964 to 1974, found that women's sex and family role attitudes have changed in the direction of egalitarianism. Similar to Parelius' (1975) findings, Mason, Czajka, and Arber (1976) found that employment and division of labor in the home were areas of significant attitudinal change between 1964 and 1970, and that after 1970 these changes toward egalitarianism continued and may, in fact, have accelerated. In contrast to Parelius'

---

[2] For an analysis of role changes during earlier periods of American history see, for example, Bridges (1965), Demos (1968 and 1970), Easton (1976), Furstenberg (1966), Gordon 1969), Gordon and Bernstein (1970), Lantz, et al. (1968, 1973, 1975, and 1977), McGovern (1968), and Welter (1966). For an excellent discussion of sex role changes during the twentieth century see Filene (1974).

(1975) study, these authors not only documented those changes that had taken place, but analyzed the possible causes of such changes. Mason, Czajka, and Arber (1976, p. 573) conclude that "educational attainment and employment are among the most important individual level predictors of attitudes."

Previous literature has also suffered from large gaps between data points. For example, Roper and LaBeff (1977) found, in replicating Kirkpatrick's (1936) study on intergenerational change in sex and family role attitudes, that there has been a "trend toward more egalitarian attitudes." However, at both time periods (1934 and 1974) parents were found to be less egalitarian in their attitudes than their children, men's attitudes were less egalitarian than women's, and, finally, both men and women were more favorable toward those aspects of sex and family equality outside the home—such as employment and politics—than the home-related issues, such as domestic responsibilities. Likewise, Roper and LaBeff (1977) confirmed Mason, Czajka, and Arber's (1976) findings that higher levels of education were associated with more egalitarian attitudes.

Obviously, more extended and chronologically complete analyses are needed to document those changes that have occurred—indeed, to document whether there has been change at all—and to provide us with additional clues as to why such changes, if any, took place. The portrayal of families in mass media advertising is one source of this needed information.

Unrepresentative sampling and potentially biased measurement

Although a number of studies have investigated sex and family roles in mass media advertising, few have taken advantage of advertising as a source of longitudinal data. Many of these studies seem to be more concerned with illustrating the "bad press" that women have received in advertising rather than with applying careful scientific analysis. By "scientific," this author means an analysis that has used the scientific method and all that it entails, such as an attempt to be objective, using a random and representative sample wherever this is possible, etc. This is not to suggest that such "unscientific" literature does not serve useful functions, for example, generating testable hypotheses and making people aware of possible sex and family role stereotyping.

Komisar (1972, p. 207), for example, in her discussion of the image of women in advertising points out that "it spews out images

of women as sex-mates, housekeepers, mothers and menial workers."
Kilbourne (1977, p. 293) is in agreement when she states that "women are shown almost exclusively as sex objects or housewives." Bardwick and Schumann (1967), in a discussion of sex and family role images in television commercials, point out that men as well as women are depicted in stereotypical roles, with women being portrayed as either sex-goddesses (if single) or eternal mothers (if married), while men are portrayed as suave, sophisticated, and sexy only when seen away from their families. In contrast, family men are seen as incompetent bumblers.

Wald's (1975) collection of advertising depicting women for the years 1865–1945 seems to suffer, particularly, from a lack of systematic analysis. The montage layout of the advertisements in Wald's collection may be pleasing to the eye, but it is confusing to those who wish to use the advertisements for an analysis of trends. Similar problems are found in Wald's (1977) analysis of advertising depicting men. Finally, Goffman (1976), in a somewhat more in-depth analysis of magazine advertising, arrives at a number of conclusions, some of which are that males are portrayed as being more authoritative and protective, while females are portrayed as being more gentle, affectionate, and dependent. However, one wonders where and how Goffman (1976) chose his sample of advertisements.

There are, however, other analyses that have used more adequate sampling and measurement techniques and that reach similar conclusions. Courtney and Lockeretz (1971), studying advertising published in 1970 general interest magazines, conclude that according to such ads: a women's place is in the home; women do not make important decisions; and women are dependent, need male protection, and are sexual playthings for men. Finally, analyses of television commercials by Courtney and Whipple (1974) and a study carried out by *Women on Words and Images* (1975) have yielded results similar to those studies involving magazine advertising. Courtney and Whipple (1974, p. 116) conclude that "women for the most part, continue to clean house, launder, cook and serve meals, while men give the orders and advice and eat the meals."

Although the above-mentioned studies have relied on more adequate sampling and measurement techniques, none of them have been longitudinal. Venkatesan and Losco (1975) provide an all too rare exception to the rule, and yet even their study covers a relatively short historical time period. They found that some of women's images in magazine ads published between 1959 and 1971 had changed, while others had remained essentially the same. The portrayal of women as sex objects, for example, had decreased since 1961, but the portrayal of women as dependent on men had remained relatively stable over the time period covered.

Overemphasis on certain family roles

Yet another deficiency within the literature has been the overemphasis on those family roles—the occupational, housework, and child-rearing roles—that we might expect to change the least, because of such factors as economic inequalities, biological circumstances, and other structural components. For example, this author (1978), in an analysis of marriage advice articles published in women's magazines between 1900 and 1974, found that, although family role prescriptions had become more egalitarian, they were still far from advocating true sexual equality in the family. A traditional differentiation of roles prevailed, with husbands primarily responsible for economic provision and wives primarily responsible for household chores and child-care. Although decision making and interpersonal support were investigated aside from the three aforementioned family roles, other equally important roles were ignored. As Nye (1976) has pointed out, there are other family roles that may experience change, such as kinship and recreational roles. These, however, have been largely ignored in research and, particularly, in the longitudinal studies.

Ignored family companionship and intimacy

Family companionship and family intimacy have likewise been ignored in the historical literature. In addition, existing research has tended to use these terms interchangeably, similar to the "family power and authority mess" discussed by Safilios-Rothschild (1970, p. 539) and others. Because of this conceptual confusion in the literature, this chaper will "lump" these terms together and discuss research relevant to companionship and/or intimacy. However, in Chapters 5 and 6 the concepts will be differentiated, and operational definitions will be provided.

If "companionship has risen to become the single most valued aspect of marriage," as Blood and Wolfe (1960, p. 150) argue, then where is the evidence for such change? Historical evidence suggests that romantic love—one component of companionship and intimacy—became an increasingly more important aspect of mate selection as we approached the end of the nineteenth century (see, for example, Lantz, et al., 1968, 1973, 1975, and 1977). However, even in terms of this component, we know little of the changes that have occurred in the twentieth century. An exception is Martel's (1968, p. 54) analysis based on family relationships in magazine fiction published between 1890 and 1955. He found a shift from the late nineteenth century where marriage was a partnership to a "growing emphasis on romance, affectuality, companionship." However, other aspects of companionship and/or intimacy remain unexplored in an historical sense. For example, are there special bonds between fathers and sons or mothers and daughters as Goffman (1976, p. 106) suggests? Has the presence of children always signaled a reduction in husband-wife companionship and/or intimacy as Rosenblatt's (1974) research might suggest? Finally, Macionis (1978), in an exploratory analysis of what he terms "intimacy,"[3] suggests that family role structure might have an influence on "intimacy," with those of more equal status being more "intimate." For example, has intimacy between husbands and wives, at least as depicted in advertisements, increased or decreased with the ever-increasing autonomy of twentieth century wives? He further suggests that family life cycle changes, with the concomitant shifts in role structure, might influence family "intimacy." However, at present, both insights lack empirical evidence.

Overemphasis on husbands and wives

Another notable deficiency in the research has been an overemphasis on husband and wife roles, accompanied by a lack of concern with the roles of other family members such as grandparents.

This overemphasis on husband and wife roles has left a number of questions unanswered. In general, there has been an overemphasis on women's roles. This limitation is particularly evident when one

---

[3] Macionis' (1978) measurement technique, which he admits is "at best, an imperfect measure of intimacy," illustrates one aspect of the conceptual confusion between intimacy and companionship. Macionis combines items concerned with *shared activity* and items concerned with *interpersonal disclosure*. From this author's perspective, the first aspect is really a measure of companionship, whereas the second aspect is more a measure of intimacy. See page 24 for a more in-depth discussion of the distinction between companionship and intimacy.

looks at the research concerning sex and family roles in advertising. Bardwick and Schumann (1967), Goffman (1976), and Wald (1977) are among the few who have bothered to study *male* sex and family roles as depicted in advertising. If there are relatively agreed-upon notions of the "ideal child," as Raina (1975) found, then have these notions gone through periods of change? If so, when and why? Has the American family become "child-centered" as Demos and Demos (1969, p. 212) suggest? Finally, the notion of the nuclear family as isolated from its extended kin has been put to rest by research that indicates that extended kin perform a number of functions in modern society. (For a review of this research, see Adams 1970.) However, when and why these functions may have changed remains a fuzzy area of family sociology.

Lack of family life cycle approach

The final limitation of the research is a deficiency common to family sociology in general: the lack of a family life cycle approach. As Hareven (1977b, p. 340) says, "families and households evolve different types of structures, organizations, and relationships, which are generally obscured in the snapshot approach." Medley's (1977, p. 9) research suggests that certain family role changes are necessary during postretirement years. Other family role adjustments also seem to be necessary as the family passes through the honeymoon, child-rearing, and empty nest stages. In addition, how do the roles of extended kin change as the family passes through its life cycle? Lastly, how does family companionship and intimacy change at specific life cycle stages?

OVERCOMING PREVIOUS LIMITATIONS

The study of family life has become increasingly popular. Our newspapers and bookstores abound with literature designed to improve family life. Television is propagating more family-related issues in documentary and entertainment formats. College courses dealing with family relationships have multiplied. Overall, one would have to conclude that the well-being of the family is of vital concern to today's American. In order to adequately meet this demand for accurate information on family life, we must rectify the shortcomings of the previous research whenever possible.

In brief, the previous research has suffered from a lack of historical evidence to document change, a disregard for how family roles change throughout the life cycle, and an overemphasis on certain family members and certain family roles. What this means for the social scientist, as well as the layman, is that they may be getting faulty information. As such, the implications can be far-reaching. Not only are the individual family members potentially influenced by this information, but so are family service agency employees.

The main contribution of the present study is its emphasis on an analysis of the *historical* and *family life cycle* changes in the *images* of family life depicted in magazine advertising published between 1920 and 1978. The longitudinal design allows us to address issues of change in family life legitimately, at least as depicted in magazine advertising. The time has come in family sociology when we must either stop talking about change, if the data do not include at least two time points (and preferably more), or we must seek out and use those data sources that make this possible.

To the extent that advertisements are a good reflection of societal values (see Chapter 2), this study allows us to deal with a number of areas of family life that until now have been largely ignored or that require further analysis. For example, this study goes beyond the usual emphasis on women's roles and looks at the historical and life cycle changes of *all* family members. In addition, questions concerning areas of family life, such as companionship and intimacy, are investigated more extensively from an historical and life cycle perspective.

In conclusion, the importance of this study can be summarized by pointing out that family sociologists have learned, often the hard way, that widely-held assumptions about the family need to be tested.

CHAPTER **II**

Images and Magazine Advertising*

THE METAMORPHOSIS OF MAGAZINE ADVERTISING

Since the initial introduction of the advertisement to the periodical, there has existed between the two industries an almost symbiotic
relationship. In its inception, however, advertising was not the strong
force it is today. "Many publishers of early American magazines were
not interested in accepting advertising for their publications." (Gaw
1961, p. 265). Rather than being popular, it was merely tolerated. As
with other business enterprises, advertising would be dependent on
industrialization and progress for its rather rapid and successful meta-
morphosis.

The high cost of publication and distribution of the late eigh-
teenth century magazine made it a "class" rather than a "mass" form
of media, a less-than-profitable undertaking for the advertiser whose
interest lay in carrying his message to the greatest number of consumers. Appeal for and attention towards the goods or services was
severely hampered by the fact that the early advertisement was liter-
ally buried in the back of a publication amid other similarly wordy
and small-type advertisements.

Towards the end of the nineteenth century and beginning of the
twentieth century, a dramatic transformation occurred in the publish-

---

*Anna and Bruce Brown coauthored this chapter.

9

ing industry—a change that would eventually lead to the "popular" magazine format. Technological advances allowed for the birth of new machinery, such as the linotype and rotary press. Even engravings, originally done by hand, were assumed mechanically by special apparatus. With the newly-founded marriage to mass production, costs of preparation and distribution decreased, resulting in ever-increasing circulation rates. Lower purchase prices of ten cents, or even five cents, boosted demand beyond expectation (Peterson 1964).

In addition to the revolution in the magazine industry itself, the revolution on the "outside" also caused quite a stir. New products and new inventions—such as our expedient automobile—required publicity. The advertiser and the manufacturer were more than happy to oblige each other through the medium of the magazine.

> Advertising, attracted by large circulations as manufacturers quested for a national market, had become virtually essential for the success of a low-priced magazine. To attract many readers, the publisher needed a low price; to maintain his low price, he needed advertising volume. And finally, magazine content had become "popular" as publishers and editors reached new audiences. (Peterson 1964, p. 13)

Through this profitable undertaking, advertisers suddenly began to concentrate on a visual arena for the sale of the product. Advertisements, once buried, were interspersed among the periodical text and printed on the larger "quarto" size pages, challenging the advertiser to focus on copy and the entire architectural design or layout of his ad. Copy—the previously wordy jumble—was decreased to give favor to the picture, either engraved or, later, in the form of photographs. Color was to become an important factor in consumer appeal, as would size of the advertisement, page position within a particular publication, and the infamous "Brand Name." With all of these factors to consider, it is not a surprise that advertising became not only a business, but also a science as well—science in the sense that marketing research was a direct outgrowth of the competition that developed through this new transformation of the advertising phenomenon.

In the early stages, marketing research consisted of little more than collecting information on the background of the consumer—social class, age, sex, marital status, etc. As the advertising industry grew, however, it became increasingly necessary to investigate such macro-level factors as birth rates, divorce rates, employment of women, etc.

Likewise, marketing research placed greater emphasis on the social-psychological motivations of the consumer. In so doing, it has become more sophisticated and more scientific to the point where

> no group of sociologists can approximate the ad teams in gathering and processing of exploitable social data. The ad teams have billions to spend annually on research and testing of reactions, and their products are magnificent accumulations of material about the shared experiences and feelings of the entire community. (McLuhan 1971, p. 229)

Within the realm of research of any nature lies the controversial issue of ethics. The advertising world has been no exception and has had its share of criticism. In their eager beginnings, advertisers did not always paint a truthful picture in their messages to the public, the result being an initially bad reputation with consumers and a skeptical reception from business colleagues. As a step to insure against attempts to deceive or defraud the public, the Curtis Advertising Code of 1910 was established with the purpose of filtering the good from the bad. Other codes have followed suit to alleviate the negative feedbacks from a process (advertising) that would somehow fail to instill public confidence; however, there has always been and still remains a controversy over whether advertisements influence the societal value system or whether they draw from it and thereby reflect it.

ADVERTISEMENTS AS A REFLECTION OF SOCIETAL VALUES

From an economic standpoint, "magazine advertising has changed the taste and habit of the population" (Wood 1956, p. 270). Over the course of its career, it has influenced freedom of press, freedom of competition, and freedom of choice. However, through the control of cost and the visual influencing of consumer buying patterns, the advertising industry can claim as its greatest achievement the raising of the economic standard of living for the populace. As such, the tremendous social influence of this enterprise cannot be ignored.

The actual role of advertising must be considered in any discussion of its effect upon society, and vice versa. In essence, the basic premise of an advertisement is to sell a product or "to convert potential consumers into actual consumers" (Millum 1975, p. 39). To be successful, an advertised message must invoke consumer reaction by first catching the reader's attention. In some instances, the bizarre or unconventional approach is employed, but, for the most part, the popular imagery—the visual panorama—has to be of a nature familiar to and consistent with prevailing cultural standards. The potential consumers must be able to "see themselves" in the social world the advertiser has constructed around the product. "Utter strangeness is just as uninteresting as complete familiarity. Total strangeness leaves the average observer at a loss" (Hepner 1941, p. 400) The instant connection is a challenge to the advertiser in that

> ...a reader's reluctance to become part of a picture which goes against his moral grain is seldom a conscious reaction. Rather it is automatic. He may turn the page... before the advertiser even has a chance to fully present his case. (Baker 1961)

Since advertising is designed for mass consumption, the advertiser is not concerned with individual values, but rather with the values of the part of the population comprising the largest segment of the buying public, i.e., the middle class. Therefore, advertising can be said to *reflect* middle-class cultural values. The shaping of cultural values is left to the few in the business of selling who "are willing to undertake the risky assignment of changing and refining public taste" (Baker 1961).

The controversy over the shaping vs. reflecting of cultural values in advertising still continues. Proponents of the shaping theory, such as Schneider (1968, p. 110), support the contention that "as modern advertising seeks to create desires, to form tastes, to influence men by their emotions, it begins to shape its own ideal of personality, its own definition of society." In the overall perspective, however, there seems to be more contribution to the hypothesis that advertising reflects values. As Lazarsfeld and Merton (1957, as cited in Fowles 1976, p. 56) point out, "the mass media of communication operate toward the maintenance of the going social and cultural structure rather than towards its change," thereby reinforcing the existing values. Lyons (1969) proposes that the most effective advertising is that which triggers the "mind-set" of the potential consumer and that "at its most effective level, mass advertising communicates precisely what the mass mind-set already believes or wants to believe" (Lyons 1969, p. 15). Furthermore, McLuhan (1964, p. 6) concludes that:

> Any expensive ad is as carefully built on the tested foundations of pub-
> lic stereotypes or "sets" of established attitudes as any skyscraper is
> built on bedrock...any acceptable ad is a vigorous dramatization of
> communal experience.

In short, the successful advertiser ascertains what potential customers want and then gives it to them.

Although there exists this orientation toward the theory that advertisements reflect cultural values, empirical support is sparse; it appears to be more an act of faith on the part of advertisers. However, in their analysis of advertising, Bauer and Greyser (1978) found that one of the reasons most often mentioned (18 percent) for liking an advertisement was that the respondent "felt I was in the situation." Likewise, the reason most often mentioned (50 percent) for finding an advertisement offensive was that it violated the respondents moral values. Evidently then, successful advertisements will not only allow the viewers to "see themselves" in the advertisement, but will also be sure to reflect the prevailing moral values. Advertisers appear to have been very successful at this, since only 5 percent of the 9,325 advertisements analyzed by Bauer and Greyser (1968) were rated as offensive.

In addition to reflecting cultural values, advertisements also reinforce existing values by repeatedly presenting these values before the public. "Advertising uses the discourse of words and images to bring about the dialogue of values" (Leymore 1975, p. viii). It is important to keep in mind that, although they reflect and reinforce existing cultural values, advertisements do not always reflect cultural reality. Cinema personalities do commercials or the commercial actor becomes a "star" in his own right; nevertheless, the consumer attempts to emulate the picture depicted. To paraphrase Millum (1975, p. 44), if advertisements did reflect reality, there would be far more pictures of slums, unattractive people, and broken-down cars than of elegant townhouses, beautiful people, and sleek new automobiles. The "common aspiration" for such items is in itself a reflection of cultural values.

A special note should be made towards the recent and controversial issue of the portrayal of women in advertising. Even as far back as the first soap advertisement, women consumers have been the focal concentration with respect to the purchase of a product. As in any message, advertisers' most effective selling tool is the creation of a conflict and/or problem, primarily through persecution or guilt. As such, it would seem that current negative criticism of women in advertisements would be justifiable. Courtney and Lockeretz's (1971, p. 94) argument that "the picture as a whole does fail to show the true range of women's roles within our society" could lend support to the contention that advertising is not a good reflection of cultural values concerning family life. Nevertheless, advertisers, in being consistent with their conservative nature, are not concerned with advocating social change; their aim is to sell a product, not to alter the status quo. In this sense, advertisements do *not* reflect what family life values "ought to be," but rather what they are at a particular point in time. As Wagner and Banos (1973, p. 214) summarize:

> While a number of critics have maintained that advertising is not moving fast enough in correctly portraying women's changing role in society, it is desirable to point out that over 50% of married women are not working outside the home and that a substantial percentage of those employed still consider their role as homemaker as important.

Historically speaking, the magazine is a "written record of American civilization" (Wood 1956, p. 374); it is a permanent and easily accessible source for the researcher. The advertisements within are preserved cultural artifacts, which, if excavated, can be of potential and unlimited use to the family sociologist. It is a fountain of information that should not be overlooked, for

> the historians and archeologists will one day discover that the ads of our times are the richest and most faithful daily reflections that any society ever made of its entire range of activities. (McLuhan 1964, p. 9)

CHAPTER **III**

Data Collection
and Analysis

ADVERTISEMENTS AS A DATA SOURCE

Two reasons for and one concern against using advertisement as data for cultural values are discussed below.

Advertisements reflect family life values

Since general interest magazines in themselves tend to conform to, rather than transform, cultural values, the advertisements contained therein are useful as history (Holder 1973, pp. 267, 277). As discussed in Chapter 2, magazine advertisements reflect cultural values concerning family life; at the same time, they do not reflect how families actually behaved, because in advertising one gets a very sterilized image of family life. For instance, children are infrequently, if ever, depicted as misbehaving. It is exactly this sterilized image of family life that can provide information on family life values as they exist at a particular time.

Advertisements avoid distortion

Parallel to Atwell's (1978, p. 2) discussion of family photographs as a data source in family sociology, the unobtrusive nature of advertisements tends to minimize distortion in the sense that "imagery gets away from recollection." In other words, relying on the memories of respondents for cultural values concerning family life at particular times in history is shaky at best. As Webb, et al. (1966, p. 111) say, "the palest ink is clearer than the best memory."

Curry and Clarke (1977, p. 21) also contend that "one of the unique strengths of using the photograph as a source of data is that it can preserve relationships." In the present study, the advertising photograph can visually preserve values concerning certain aspects of family life that are either too personal, too threatening, or simply below one's conscious level. As Goffman (1976, p. 91) states, "in advertised worlds . . . we can look in on almost everything."

As opposed to many other sources of information, such as the use of respondents in survey research or subjects in observation and experimental research, the advertisement "is there, static, and available for scrutiny and rescrutiny at any time" (Millum 1975, p. 53). It allows for the relatively easy rechecking of data already collected and for the gathering of additional information, if necessary.

Advertising law

When dealing with advertisements as a reflection of family life values, a potential problem arises in that mass communication advertising has been regulated by the Federal Trade Commission since 1914. It is conceivable, therefore, that prohibiting the advertising of some products of banning the display of certain activities might influence the image of family life depicted. After examining several works on advertising law, including Gillmor and Barron (1969), it is this author's contention that, for the most part, the Federal Trade Commission's concern has been with false and misleading advertising and not with regulating the types of products or activities exhibited. As Carol J. Jennings, attorney for the Division of Advertising Practices of the Federal Trade Commission said in a letter to this author:

> I know of no federal statutes or regulations which prohibit the advertising of any products or services that can be obtained legally. Until recently, some states have prohibited the advertising of such things as contraceptives, prescription drug prices, ophthalmic goods and services, and legal services. With regard to . . . what kinds of activities can be depicted in print advertising, these are matters left to the discretion of individual publications. (July, 1978).

Efforts to obtain information on either the written or the unwritten advertising standards of the magazines used in the present study proved unsuccessful. Based on the aforementioned information, this author contends that regulation of advertising at either the federal or state level, or by magazine editors, does not pose any significant distortion of family life values as depicted in magazine advertising, with the exception of state regulations against the advertising of contraceptives.

THE SAMPLE OF ADVERTISEMENTS

Advertisements published after 1920 were chosen for a number of reasons. First, as Chafe (1972, p. viii) points out, "the period after 1920, in particular, has been largely ignored by historians." Second, and from a more methodological perspective, the post-1920 time period was chosen because it was not until after 1914 that advertising became an established and integral part of the mass-circulation magazine format.

Selection of magazines

General interest magazines, rather than specialty magazines, were used since they are more likely to reflect a wider range of family life. Women's magazines were not included because, as Courtney and Lockeretz (1971, p. 93) point out, "they are directed primarily toward women as housewives, whatever their other roles." Figure 3.1 illustrates the middle-class, general interest magazines used and the years sampled from each magazine. Morgan and Leahy (1934), in their analysis of the "cultural content" of several general interest magazines, rated each of the magazines used in the present research as middle class. There were three different magazines from which advertisements were selected for each year under investigation, with the exception of 1920. This helped to assure that any differences in the images of family life were a result of changes over time and not simply differences in the editorial policies of specific magazines.

Criteria for selecting advertisements

The only advertisements used in the analysis were those in which it was obvious that family members are represented. One might pose the question: "How do we know that it is a family scene that is being depicted." The answer is that if it is important to the advertiser to

Figure 3.1.   Magazines Sampled by Year.

make such a message clear, then he will do so either verbally or non-verbally. As Goffman (1976, pp. 83, 91) asserts, "the point about an ad is what its composer meant us to infer as to what is going on: . . . ads are intentionally choreographed to be unambiguous." Or as Up-degroff (1972, p. 20) affirms, "great advertisements are always sim-ple—always obvious." The point is that because of the unambiguous and obvious nature of advertising, viewers of advertisements "know" what is a family scene and what is not. They are subjective judgments made by viewers based upon the total configuration of the advertise-ment. However, in addition to these subjective interpretations, there are objective clues that viewers either consciously or unconsciously employ in their judgments. For example, the presence of wedding rings, children, intimate apparel such as pajamas and underwear, fam-ily rituals such as shared meals and visiting, and personal activities such as bathing and sleeping are all used to indicate a family scene. Likewise, the text of an advertisement often contains explicit state-ments concerning the family relationship of those depicted. To re-iterate, it is the gestalt of all these clues that forms the basis of the viewers' judgments. It is this author's contention that viewers of advertisements are extremely accurate in these judgments. In order to substantiate this contention, three magazine issues were coded by both the author and another trained coder in terms of which adver-tisements depicted family scenes, the results yielding inter-coder agreement on 100 percent of the advertisements.

Selection of advertisements

All advertisements that were published during every fifth year between 1920 and 1977, which met the above criteria, were tabulated.
The year 1931 was substituted for 1930 and the year 1936 was substituted for 1935 due to the unavailability of certain magazines. This
resulted in a total of 1,489 advertisements. From this tabulation, a
simple random sample was chosen of ten advertisements for each of
the five family life cycle changes (see page 21 for a discussion of
these stages), for each of the 13 years under investigation. This resulted in a potential sample of 650 advertisements. In actuality, due
primarily to difficulties in obtaining advertisements depicting the
postparental family life cycle stage, a total of 521 advertisements
comprised the final sample. Table 3.1 indicates the total number of
advertisements sampled by year and by family life cycle stage. (See
Tables 3.2, 3.3, and 3.4 for the percentage of advertisements by magazine, year, and family life cycle, stage, respectively).

Table 3.1.
**Number of Advertisements Sampled by Year and Family
Life Cycle**

| | Family Life Cycle Stage | | | | | |
Year	1	2	3	4	5	Total
1920	10	10	8	10	2	40
1925	10	10	10	10	9	49
1931	10	10	6	10	3	39
1936	10	10	6	10	3	39
1940	10	10	4	10	0	34
1945	10	10	8	10	1	39
1950	10	10	10	10	5	45
1955	10	10	10	10	2	42
1960	10	10	10	10	10	50
1965	10	9	10	10	6	45
1970	10	10	6	10	1	37
1975	10	5	2	10	1	28
1977	10	6	6	10	2	34
Total	130	120	96	130	45	521

Table 3.2.
Frequency and Percentage of Advertisements by Magazine

Magazine	Absolute Frequency	Percentage
American	173	33.2
Life	137	26.3
Time	120	23.0
Saturday Evening Post	46	8.8
Newsweek	45	8.6
Total	521	99.9

Table 3.3.
Frequency and Percentage of Advertisements by Year

Year	Absolute Frequency	Percentage
1920	40	7.7
1925	49	9.4
1931	39	7.5
1936	39	7.5
1940	34	6.5
1945	39	7.5
1950	45	8.6
1955	42	8.1
1960	50	9.6
1965	45	8.6
1970	37	7.1
1975	28	5.4
1977	34	6.5
Total	521	100.0

THE CODING OF THE ADVERTISEMENTS

Both the verbal and the nonverbal components of the advertise-ments were used in the content analysis. Each of the advertisements was analyzed in terms of the variables discussed below. Since all of

Table 3.4.
Frequency and Percentage of Advertisements by
Family Life Cycle

Life Cycle Stage	Absolute Frequency	Percentage
1	130	25.0
2	121	23.2
3	94	18.0
4	131	25.1
5	45	8.6
Total	521	99.9

the coding was done by the author, an initial check of inter-rater reliability was made. Both another trained coder and the author coded 20 advertisements in order to pinpoint any necessary methodological changes before the actual content analysis was begun.

Historical time

This variable was measured by simply tabulating the year when the advertisement was published.

Family life cycle

"The life cycle of the family is a term that has been used for too many years in reference to the succession of critical stages through which the typical family passes during its life span" (Glick 1977, p. 5). As mentioned in Chapter 1, the family life cycle has been neglected too often as an independent variable in family research. Hareven (1977a, p. 58) aptly discusses the importance of the family life cycle perspective.

> Social scientists have often studied the family as a monolithic institution. In reality, the family is in constant flux. It is the scene of interaction between various fluid individual lives. Individual transitions into and out of different family roles, such as leaving home, getting married, setting up an independent household, commencement of parenthood, or—at the other end of the cycle—widowhood, are interrelated with the changes in the family as a collective unit.

In the present study, the family life cycle was a central independent variable in its own right, but it was also used in conjunction with the historical passage of time. In other words, it is not enough to investigate changes in family life values over the family life cycle or over historical time. The present study went one step further by investigating historical changes in the effects of the family life cycle on family life values, and vice versa.

Due to the nature of the data source used in this study, the following family life cycle stages (which were easy to identify) were used:

1. Married, no children (preparental).
2. Married, all children under six.
3. Married, combination of children under and over six.
4. Married, all children over six.
5. Married, no children at home (postparental).

This typology suffers from some of the same limitations of most stage models of the family, since it is based on the conventional script of a marriage that bears children and survives until old age. In addition, it suffers from a lack of emphasis on the timing of family stage changes. However, due to the nature of the data source, this seemed the best alternative. For an in-depth discussion of these limitations, see Elder (1977).

Each stage indicates a change in family structure. Age composition of the children is emphasized in stages two through four because certain configurations allow for greater potential participation by children in aspects of family life, such as family roles, companionship, and intimacy. For example, if all the children are under six, then it is assumed that it becomes one or both of the parents' responsibility to provide care for them; however, a family where some of the children are under six and some are older, possibly teenagers, allows for the sharing of child-rearing by parents and older siblings. The age of the husband and wife was used to discriminate between preparental (stage 1) and postparental (stage 5) families.

Number of male and female children

The number of male and female children depicted in the advertisement was tabulated in an effort to see if differing numbers and sexual composition of children might have an effect on aspects of family life, such as family roles, companionship, and intimacy. For example, in terms of children, Glick (1977, p. 11) explains that:

> Growing up in a family of four children is quite different in many ways from growing up in one of two children. The larger the family, the larger the proportion of time the children are likely to spend interacting with one another, whereas the smaller the family, the greater the proportion of time the children are likely to spend interacting with their parents.

Family roles

The present research analyzed the roles of all family members, including extended kin, as opposed to analyzing sex roles, which emphasize male versus female issues. The *qualitative* aspect of coding this variable involved verbally specifying in detail the activity in which the family member was engaged. The *quantitative* coding involved assigning the appropriate numerical value in terms of the "family role code" listed below. The statistical analysis of this variable involved computing the proportion of advertisements that depicted a particular family member in a particular family role. For example, what was the proportion of advertisements that depicted grandmothers engaged in child-care in 1920, 1925, etc.? It should be noted that one particular person in the advertisement can fill several family positions. For example, an adult male can fill the positions of husband (in relation to his wife), father (in relation to his children), and son (in relation to his parents). The "Family Role Code" used is as follows:

0 = Personal care
1 = Economic provision
2 = Household task
3 = Child-care
4 = Recreation
5 = Therapeutic
6 = Buying
7 = Gift-giving
8 = Indeterminate
9 = Family member not depicted

Companionship

This variable measured those family activities that were shared and indicated which family members shared in these activities. Although the specific activity was *qualitatively* indicated, such as riding a bike, feeding an infant, cooking, etc., the following categories of potentially shared activities were used to structure the *quantitative* coding of companionship: economic provision, household tasks, child-care, recreation, therapeutic, buying, and gift-giving. The quantitative coding involved assigning a numerical value that corresponded to a particular combination of family members sharing in the activity. The statistical analysis of this variable involved computing the proportion of advertisements that depicted particular family members sharing particular activities. For example, what was the proportion of advertisements that depicted grandmothers and grandfathers sharing in child-care in 1920, 1925, etc.?

Intimacy

Intimacy in family life is closely aligned with the issue of companionship; it differs, however, from the latter in the sense that companionship, as used in this analysis at least, necessarily implies shared activity of some kind, whereas intimacy does not. For example, a husband and wife may share the activity of watching television together (companionship), but may do so by sitting in separate chairs (less intimate) or closely holding each other (more intimate). Similarly, they may be engaged in separate activities: the husband watching television and the wife reading a book (lack of companionship) in either the same room (more intimate) or in separate rooms (less intimate).

This variable was measured by drawing on one of the basic premises of Levinger and Gunner's (1967) "interpersonal grid," that premise being that the horizontal distance between persons is a measure of intimacy. As Argyle (1975, p. 311) states, "the degree of liking felt toward another is communicated by physical closeness." Several studies (Carlson and Price 1966, Little 1965) have empirically supported the validity of this measure.

The "family intimacy index" presented below was used to code this variable. The choice of distances designated for each level of intimacy is adapted from the work of Hall (1959). Because of scaling problems, the determination of the physical distance between family members in the advertisements was not based on actual measured units, but rather on subjective evaluations by the author. However, a test of inter-rater reliability carried out on 25 advertisements produced agreement on 96 percent of the intimacy scores assigned. It should be noted that there is disagreement in the literature regarding physical distance as a measure of intimacy, or of status, or of both. For example, Sommer (1961) and, later, Lott and Sommer (1967), using physical distance as a measure of status, found that those of unequal status were placed further apart at tables, while peers were seated closer together. However, in support of the physical distance equals intimacy argument, Mehrabian (1969, p. 363) points out that:

> Sommer's (1967) review of status relationships and spatial arrangements suggested that perhaps bodily orientation of communicators, rather than the distance between them, is a more important variable for the communication of status relationships.

The "family intimacy index" used is as follows:

1 = Nonintimate (four feet or more between each other).
2 = Intimate (within four feet of each other, but not touching each other).
3 = Very intimate (touching each other).

QUALITATIVE AND QUANTITATIVE ANALYSIS

According to Fogel (1975, p. 333) in his article on the limits of quantitative methods in history:

> The majority probably hold with Arthur Schlesinger, Jr. that "almost all important questions are important precisely because they are not susceptible to quantitative answers."

Certainly there has been strong resistance by historians to the introduction of quantitative methods into their discipline, but Schlesinger (1962, p. 770) goes too far. (For a discussion of this resistance, see Rutman 1973.) Implicit in his statement is the notion that all historical questions that are susceptible to quantitative methods are unimportant.

Sociologists generally lean toward the other extreme, with an emphasis on quantification. Of course, neither the strict qualitative

researcher nor the strict quantitative researcher is correct if he blind-
ly refuses to admit that each method has its advantages and disadvan-
tages, as well as separate research questions to which each is best
suited.

In the present study, both a qualitative and a quantitative approach were used. An example will illustrate the importance of using
both methods whenever possible. A strictly *quantitative* analysis of
these advertisements indicated that fathers since 1920 were increasingly depicted in child-care. Furthermore, even though this is a nominal level variable, the use of dummy variables made it possible to esti-
mate the strength and statistical significance of this relationship, something that would be quite impossible with qualitative data. However,
it was only with the use of *qualitative* data that it became evident
that fathers were increasingly depicted in only certain aspects of
child-care, in particular, the play aspects as opposed to the physical
care aspects. In short, *quantitative* data is necessary for the purposes
of statistical analysis, but this must be weighed against the inevitable
loss of information. *Qualitative* data, on the other hand, is rich in de-
scriptive information, but lacks the ability to be analyzed statistically. Therefore to reiterate, both approaches should be used whenever possible.

Statistical analysis

When choosing appropriate statistical techniques, the issue of
levels of measurement is of central concern. Below are listed the levels
of measurement for the variables in the present study:

Variable	*Level of Measurement*
Historical time	Interval
Family life cycle	Ordinal
Number of male children	Ratio
Number of female children	Ratio
Family roles	Nominal
Family companionship	Nominal
Family intimacy	Ordinal

Certain statistical techniques are appropriate to use with variables
at certain levels of measurement. For instance, Pearson's correlation
coefficient is, strictly speaking, to be used only with variables that
are at least interval level or better. It is precisely this issue of strict-

ness that is of concern to Labovitz (1972) in his discussion of the "sacred cows and rituals" in sociological use of statistical techniques.

Labovitz (1972) makes two points pertinent to the statistical analysis in the present study. First, he suggests that nominal level variables be reconceptualized in order to raise them to ordinal level, thus allowing the use of more powerful statistical techniques. Whether or not this can be done with all nominal level variables is another question, but the point here is to discuss why this author reconceptualizes family life cycle as an ordinal rather than a nominal level variable.

Some may view the measurement of family life cycle stages as being of nominal level. After all, is there a mathematical relationship between the different stages? Does a family in the postparental stage have more of whatever it is that is being measured than a family in the preparental stage? Taking into consideration Labovitz's (1972, p. 22) suggestion to reconceptualize nominal level variables in order to raise them to ordinal level, this author can answer "yes" to the questions above. Families at later stages of the family life cycle have passed through *more* stages than families at earlier stages.

The second suggestion Labovitz (1972, p. 23) makes pertinent to the present study is to treat ordinal level variables as though they were interval level, again allowing the use of "more powerful, sensitive, better developed, and interpretable statistics." This can be done because certain statistical techniques are robust; that is, they maintain their logically deduced interpretations even when their assumptions have been violated (Labovitz 1972, p. 19). However, see Mayer (1971) for a discussion of the dangers of treating ordinal level data as interval data.

Briefly, the following routines—Cross-Tabulation, Breakdown, and Analysis of Variance (available on the computer program, SPSS, Statistical Package for the Social Sciences)—were used in the statistical analysis. The purpose of this analysis was to determine the presence, strength, and significance of relationships between the independent variables (historical time, family life cycle stage, number of male children, and number of female children) and the dependent variables (family roles, family companionship, and family intimacy). More specific details will be given in later chapters concerning the techniques that were actually used for analyzing the relationships between the aforementioned variables.

Mention should be made, however, about what this author considers to be a major contribution of this study. The primary thrust of this research was to analyze changes in the depiction of family roles, companionship, and intimacy in magazine advertising over time and over the family life cycle. This in itself is an important contribution to the literature because of the general lack of an historical and family life cycle approach to these aspects of family life. In addition, through the use of analysis of variance, the *separate* effects of historical time were able to be investigated while holding family life cycle stage constant, and vice versa. For example, the present study was not only concerned with changes in the image of husband-wife intimacy since 1920 or with changes in the images of husband-wife intimacy over the family life cycle. It was also concerned with changes in the image of husband-wife intimacy over the family life cycle since 1920 and with changes in the image of husband-wife intimacy since 1920 at specific family life cycle stages. Elder (1977) speaks to this issue in part when he says that to understand the impact of historical change on family life, it is important to know how this change affects families at different life cycle stages.

CHAPTER ***IV***

Family Roles

Without question, family roles at present are very much the "in" topic of discussion among sociologists. As such, any family researcher interested in this aspect of scientific investigation runs the risk of criticism on two bases: one, of jumping on the bandwagon and two, of restating previous results born of different data sources. This author wishes to fend off any accusations in this direction. As to the latter criticism, one could justify the present study as an example of triangulation as a method of validation. With respect to the former criticism, new input into any inquiry could yield fresh information (as was the case in the present study); scientific research would make little progress without constant professional reevaluation.

Along the line of new ideas generated, specific findings will be presented and discussed, even if they were not significant at the "sacred .05 level." A clarification of this approach is necessary. First, there is often something quite significant about nonsignificant findings, particularly if they go against established theory. This is not to say that established theory should be discarded simply based on one study. Rather, these nonsignificant findings serve a useful purpose in bringing about a more critical evaluation of established theory. Second, in research dealing with change over time, the lack of change is often significant. Third, as Labovitz (1968, p. 221) points out, in research "exploring a set of interrelations for the purpose of developing hypotheses to be tested in another study, a larger error rate will tend to yield more hypotheses." In other words, one does not want to bury potential hypotheses at the early stages of a research project simply

because they fail to reach the "sacred .05 level" of significance. Therefore, those findings considered "important" will be presented; if they
are significant at the .05 level or better, they will be discussed as such.

The remainder of this chapter will focus on a discussion of the
activities that family members were depicted engaging in and how
this depiction may have changed since 1920 and over the family life
cycle. In order to avoid repetition, the phrase "as depicted in magazine advertising" will be taken as a given when referring to the findings.[1]

WIVES

Economic provision

Not surprisingly, wives were scarcely depicted in economic provision. The ideology that a married woman's place is in the home was
reflected in these advertisements—of the 521 advertisements analyzed, only five portrayed working wives. Four of the five appeared
in 1931 during the Depression, a time when it became an economic
necessity for a wife to work. In addition, it is interesting to note that
the jobs these wives held allowed them to remain at home, so as not
to interfere with their other duties such as child-care and housework.
For example, advertisements told wives that they could *supplement*
their husband's income by selling homemade candy and doughnuts
to neighbors and friends. The values reflected in these advertisements are consistent with the behavior of working wives for the general time period around the 1930s. As Rollins (1963, p. 226) points
out, in 1920 only 7.5 percent of the employed wives were working
for money outside of their homes.

To further illustrate the notion that employment for married
women should not interfere with other home-bound duties, none of
these five advertisements were of families at the second stage of the
family life cycle, that is, when children are all under six years of age.
Social scientists have been struggling since at least the 1950s with the
question of whether children of employed mothers are affected in any

---

[1] Tables discussed in this chapter can be found in Appendix A.

detrimental way. As a culture we seem hesitant to accept evidence that suggests that there are no detrimental effects from mother employment per se. In other words, we continue to emphasize the importance of the "mother-child" bond in our value system, regardless of the fact that "the largest recent increase in labor force activity has occurred for . . . mothers of preschool children" (Waite 1976, p. 65).

How can this contradiction between actual behavior and cultural values expressed in advertising be explained? One possibility is that although the proportion of working wives has steadily increased since the turn of the century, cultural values, particularly those dealing with working mothers of preschool children, have lagged behind.

Household tasks

A role with which wives were intimately involved was housework. Regardless of the housework activity involved, be it cooking, cleaning, shopping, decorating, etc., the wife was depicted because the home operation was primarily her responsibility. She was there essentially to meet the needs of other family members. One gets the impression, by looking at their smiles, that these wives do their housework prompted by a loving concern for their husbands and children.

The proportion of advertisements depicting wives involved in housework has decreased significantly since 1920, as can be seen in Figure 4.1. However, the decrease has not been consistent. A peak year occurred in 1920, possibly as a result of the remnants of the Victorian era with its emphasis on domesticity as a mark of the "true woman." Other peak years were 1945 and 1960, possibly an indication of the nation's desire to return to normalcy after the Second World War and the Korean War.

Overall, however, wives have been decreasingly depicted in the role of housewife. This finding is consistent with Nye's (1976, p. 99) assertion that housekeeping is a declining family role, but is contrary to the fact that wives continue to spend as many hours per week on housework as they did at the turn of the century, regardless of the technological advances in household appliances (see Bose 1978 for an excellent discussion of this phenomenon). One reason for this contradiction between cultural values and the actual behavior of wives deals with the devaluing of the housewife role over the century. The phrase "just a housewife" is indicative of the lack of prestige attached

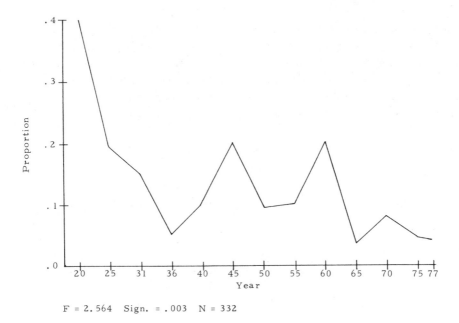

F = 2.564   Sign. = .003   N = 332

Figure 4.1.   Proportion of Advertisements Depicting Household
Tasks by Wives, by Year.

to this form of work; therefore, regardless of the fact that wives still find themselves taking on most of the household tasks, the cultural values have shifted and, at least in advertising, this activity of wives is being deemphasized.

According to Lopata (1966), the wife's role in housework goes through a sequence of stages that correspond to different family life cycle stages. The first stage is referred to as the "becoming a housewife" stage. This is marked both by learning how to perform the housewife duties and also by internalizing this role as part of the wife's self-concept. From a structural-functional perspective, advertising may perform an important service by emphasizing housework at family life cycle stage one, that is preparental, thereby providing new wives with the media role models to emulate. In fact, it was the preparental stage that evidenced the most emphasis on the wife's role in housework. Thereafter, there was a decreasing emphasis on the wife's role in housework over the family life cycle. Nevertheless, the fact that this decrease is not statistically significant indicates that housework remains an integral part of the wife's role throughout the family life cycle (Table A.1).

Although the depiction of wives engaged in housework has decreased significantly since 1920, is it possible that these changes have occurred only for wives at certain family life cycle stages? Analysis of variance indicates that this decrease is most evident for the first three life cycle stages, that is, either when there are no children or when there are still preschool children present (2-way interaction, F = 1.420, p = .048). The depiction of wives at family life cycle stages four and five has not evidenced this decrease, essentially remaining constant since 1920. Therefore, it is the younger wife in particular whose role in housework has decreased in coverage in magazine advertising.

Therapeutics

Nye (1976, p. 111) defines the therapeutic role as one that involves "assisting the spouse to cope with and, hopefully, dispose of the problem with which he is confronted." In the present study, advertisements showing family members comforting, sympathizing, or actively assisting another family member with a problem were coded in terms of the therapeutic role.[2] For example, an advertisement for a backache relief product showed a wife rubbing ointment into the husband's back.

How have wives fared in terms of the therapeutic role? Figure 4.2 indicates that since 1920 there have been significant but irregular changes. The wife's role in therapeutic activities is *relatively* obscure before 1931 but then shoots up dramatically only to return to pre-Depression levels in 1936. After 1936, this role for wives is essentially ignored for the remainder of the century.

Although only eight of the 332 advertisements depicting wives showed them in this therapeutic capacity, it is this very absence that brings into question Nye's (1976, p. 111) assertion that the thera-

---

[2] Therapeutic activities performed by a parent for a child were coded under the separate category of child-care.

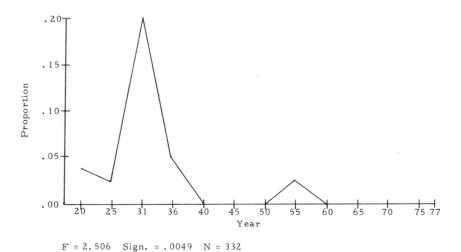

F = 2.506   Sign. = .0049   N = 332

Figure 4.2.   Proportion of Advertisements Depicting Therapeutic
Activities by Wives, by Year.

peutic role is emerging in American culture. If it is, then it is certainly not evident in magazine advertising. A more plausible explanation
of this lack of emphasis on therapeutic activities in advertisements
hinges upon the "sterilized" view of family life presented in advertising. Advertisements tend to shy away from the more disruptive aspects of family life; therefore, the potential for therapeutic activity
by wives is decreased.

In terms of family life cycle changes and wives' involvement in
therapeutic activities, Figure 4.3 indicates a significant curvilinear
relationship. Wives are depicted as being much more involved in such
activities in relationship to their husbands during the preparental
and, particularly, the postparental stages. It seems that when children
come on the scene, wives are less likely to be therapeutic towards
husbands, no doubt because of their increased involvement in child-
care.

Recreation

According to Orthner (1975, p. 91), "there has been a shift in
values toward acceptance of leisure as a legitimate . . . life goal." The
present analysis indicates that, for wives, recreation has been given
significantly increased attention in advertising since 1920 (Figure
4.4). Not surprisingly, a low point occurred during the Depression
years, when the portrayal of wives engaged in leisure activities would

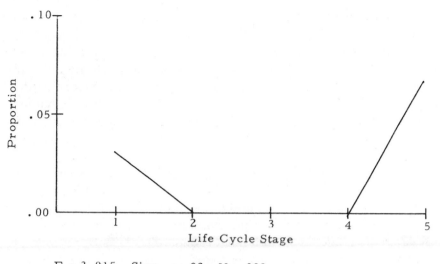

F = 3.015   Sign. = .03   N = 332

Figure 4.3. Proportion of Advertisements Depicting Therapeutic Activities by Wives, by Family Life Cycle.

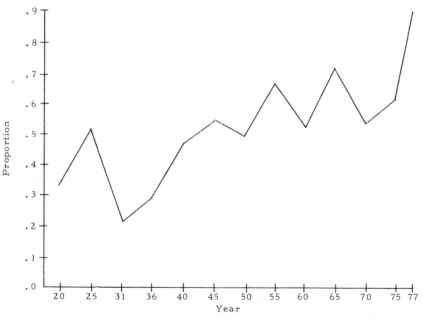

F = 3.693   Sign. = .00   N = 332

Figure 4.4. Proportion of Advertisements Depicting Recreation by Wives, by Year.

have been more likely to have been viewed as frivolous and irresponsible.

What sort of recreational activities are wives depicted in? For most of the time period, wives are shown in what might be called the more "home-bound" activities such as reading, knitting, and gardening. However, around 1975, probably due in part to the feminist movement and the "back to nature" fad, there was a dramatic shift to more active recreational activities such as hiking, tennis, camping, fishing, and swimming.

Looking at family life cycle changes, advertisements stress recreation for wives throughout the life cycle, but there is, nonetheless, a nonsignificant increase over the family life cycle with high points at stages four and five, when all the children are either over six years of age or are no longer living at home (Table A.2).

The number of children was found to have an *inverse* effect on the likelihood of wives being depicted in recreational activities (Table A.3). Given the fact that there was a significant *direct* relationship between family life cycle and the number of children, the fact that wives at later stages of the family life cycle were more likely to be depicted in recreational activities would seem to be a contradiction. However, it must be remembered that the relationship between family life cycle and the depiction of wives engaged in recreational activities was not statistically significant. Therefore, the inverse effects of the increasing number of children over the family life cycle may be offset by the increased freedom wives experience as they relinquish child-care responsibilities as children grow older.

Why there is less emphasis on recreation for wives at the preparental stage is not clear, especially since, as Orthner (1975, p. 101) points out, both husbands and wives view leisure activities as critical to marital satisfaction at this stage of the family life cycle. An answer to this question may be supplied by looking at whether it is only during certain family life cycle stages that wives have been increasingly depicted in recreational activities since 1920. Analysis of variance results indicate that, although there is a general increase for all stages, the most dramatic increase occurred during the preparental stage. Therefore, there is a significant interaction effect (F = 1.735, p = .004) between historical time and family life cycle. The emphasis Orthner's (1975) present day respondents place on recreation during the preparental stage may have gone through an evolution since 1920, at least as depicted in advertising.

HUSBANDS

Economic provision

Similar to the emphasis placed upon household task performance for the wife, the cultural values expressed in magazine advertising have made it very clear that it is the husband's responsibility to support the family financially. Husbands are not only portrayed working, but are also shown investing their money and taking part in forced savings plans through their place of employment. The message behind these ads is that "your family is depending on you for financial security." This, of course, is not a message that is communicated to husbands just through the mass media; it is also built into the legal system. Weitzman (1975, p. 534) points out, for example, that:

> A wife is never held responsible for the support of her husband in two-thirds of the states, and in the remaining minority of states, a wife is held responsible for her husband's support only if he has become incapacitated or a public charge.

This emphasis in advertising on the husband's responsibility to provide financially has not, however, been constant since 1920. Essentially, as indicated in Figure 4.5, there have been three peaks: one in 1920, one in 1936, and the other in 1970. One of the two low-points comes in 1945 and is easily explained by the fact that the "work" for men at this time was still being thought of largely in terms of national defense. One common factor that may explain the emphasis on employment for husbands during 1936 and 1970 is simply the fact that the former was a period of economic depression and the latter a period of economic recession. In this sense, financial provision was on the minds of the populace and may simply have made good advertising copy, therefore, reflecting cultural values.

Along with the idea of husbands being responsible for providing financially for their families, it is interesting to note that most of this emphasis was placed upon husbands depicted in family life cycle stage two, when all children are under six years of age (Figure 4.6). No doubt this is when many husbands begin truly to experience the pressure of financial responsibilities—when children first come on the scene. Advertisements reflect this concern of young husbands beginning families. After this peak at stage two, there was a significant decrease in the emphasis placed on the husband's role in economic pro-

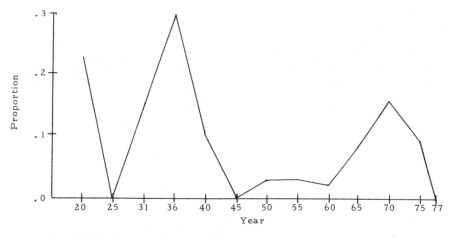

F = 2.793   Sign. = .001   N = 332

Figure 4.5.   Proportion of Advertisements Depicting Economic Provision by Husbands, by Year.

vision. At the postparental stage, this aspect of the husband's role was essentially ignored, indicating that at least one of the main motivations for husbands working, that is, supporting children, no longer operates. Of course, advertisements at the postparental stage emphasized the benefits to be gained by having prepared financially for retirement, but the message was always that this was a responsibility that ought to have been met at earlier stages of the family life cycle.

Regarding whether the emphasis on economic provision for husbands during times of economic depression (1936) or economic recession (1970) was evident for husbands at all family life cycle stages, analysis of variance indicates that there was a similar peak during these two time periods for husbands at all stages except the postparental. Given the absence of children, even an economic depression is seen as relatively less of a dilemma.

Household tasks

The data (Table A.4) indicate that, in general, husbands are rarely pictured doing housework, and as Goffman (1976, p. 105) adds, those that are are often portrayed as inept. Two reasons may serve to explain this "bumbling husband portrayal." First, in our culture housework is not seen as an integral part of the husband's role. Second, it may be that because housework has been such an integral part of the wife's role, although decreasingly so, that the cultural values, similar to wives' actual behavior (Safilios-Rothschild 1972, p. 65), are hesitant to allow husbands to become too involved in what is essentially considered "women's work."

Although both Ballweg (1967) and Kerckhoff (1964) found that husbands take on increased responsibilities for household tasks after retirement, the present analysis did not find a similar increase in the emphasis on this role for husbands in the postparental family life cycle stage (Table A.5). Of course, retirement and postparental are not equivalent concepts, but even among the advertisements that indicated that the husband was retired, there was no noticeable increase in the participation of husbands in housework.

One would have also expected an increase at this stage based on Powell's (1963, p. 232) finding that husbands in families with adoles-

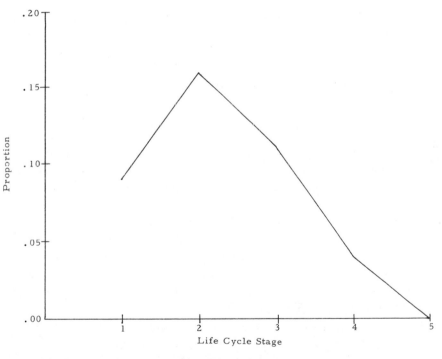

F = 2.416   Sign. = .04   N = 332

Figure 4.6.   Proportion of Advertisements Depicting Economic Provision by Husbands, by Family Life Cycle.

cent children did less housework because these older children "took up the slack." When the adolescent children are gone, in the post-parental stage, one might expect husbands to assume responsibility. Such is not the case, at least as reflected in advertising. Actually, comparisons across different stages of the family life cycle may be quite meaningless based on the present data, since there is a highly insignificant relationship between the depiction of husbands engaged in housework and family life cycle. Overall, one would conclude that since 1920 housework for husbands has not been an essential part of their role, regardless of the family life cycle stage.

Therapeutics

Similar to the lack of emphasis placed upon therapeutic activity for wives, there was even less emphasis on this activity for husbands. Of the 332 advertisements portraying husbands, only two (1931 and 1940) involved husbands in this capacity. Taking into account the limited number of cases (eight for wives and two for husbands), the fact that wives were portrayed more often in therapeutic activities than were husbands seems consistent with Levinger's (1964, p. 447) finding that wives initiate socially supportive interaction more often.

In terms of family life cycle changes, again the low number of cases makes it impossible to draw any substantial conclusion. Nevertheless, the fact that the two advertisements depicting husbands in this role both occur in families in the preparental stage parallels the findings for wives; that is, husbands and wives, although infrequently portrayed in therapeutic activities in relationship to each other, are *never* depicted in this capacity when children are on the scene.

Recreation

Recreation has become an increasingly important aspect of the husband's role, just as it has for the wife. As can be seen in Figure 4.7, since 1920 there has been a significant increase in the portrayal of husbands engaged in recreation. The low points in the portrayal of this activity occurred during the Depression years of 1931 and 1936, when recreation by husbands may have been looked upon as frivolous and irresponsible.

Although there were no significant differences in the depiction of husbands engaged in recreation over the family life cycle, it is the fourth stage, when all children are over six years of age, that evidenced the greatest emphasis on recreation (Table A.6). It may well be that

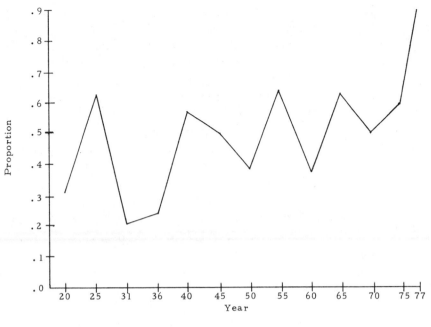

F = 4.534   Sign. = .00   N = 332

Figure 4.7.   Proportion of Advertisements Depicting Recreation by
Husbands, by Year.

at this stage both spouses have the increased time and freedom to devote to recreation, thanks to the education system taking over much
of the responsibility for child-care, and also the family having more
income as compared to earlier stages.

Again, like the wives' involvement in recreation, the number of
children was found to have an *inverse* effect on the recreation of husbands (Table A.3). Since there is a significant increase in the number
of children throughout the family life cycle, the fact that husbands
are more often depicted in recreation at stage four may seem to be a
contradiction. However, the inverse effects of the increasing number
of children may be offset by the fact that older children may rely
less on their father for recreation, thereby freeing his time for personal recreational activities.

Until 1960, husbands were portrayed in more sedentary forms of
recreation such as gardening, reading, listening to the radio, and viewing television. Afterwards, husbands were more likely to be biking,
playing tennis, skiing, sailing, camping, etc. This trend may be indic-

ative of the emphasis on physical fitness, which started during the Kennedy years and has continued since.

The fact that the more active forms of recreation were stressed earlier for husbands (1960) than for wives (1975) is indicative of the notion that men are more athletic than women. In fact, it may be that recreation in general has been thought of as a more important component of the husband's role than the wife's throughout the life cycle. Analysis of variance indicated that the increased emphasis on recreation for husbands since 1920 is evident and about equally strong for all family life cycle stages with the exception of stage three (2-way interactions, F = 1.454, p = .037). Wives, on the other hand, showed the least dramatic increases in emphasis on recreation in advertisements depicting families at the last two stages of the family life cycle (2-way interactions, F = 1.735, p = .004).

MOTHERS

Child-care

In advertising since 1920, the mother has been primarily responsible for child-care. The reason for this emphasis on females as child-caretakers stems in large part from popular notions concerning the basic nature of women. Many believed women were naturally better "mothers" than men; even today the issue continues to be a question for debate. Talk of "mother instinct" and similar concepts have been drawn upon to explain and legitimize this responsibility.

No matter how important child-care may have been to the women's role in the family, it has been significantly less emphasized in advertising since 1920 (as seen in Figure 4.8). Surprisingly, the greatest emphasis on child-care appeared in 1931, at a time when the birth rate was at one of its lowest points. Possibly, this emphasis can be explained by the prevailing attitude of the early 1930s, which suggested that married women ought to be at home rather than employed and, as such, taking jobs away from men who "really needed them." The "baby boom" years show no dramatic increase in the emphasis on child-care, although they are higher than subsequent years. The shift away from defining a woman's role in the family largely in terms of motherhood can best explain this decrease in emphasis over time.

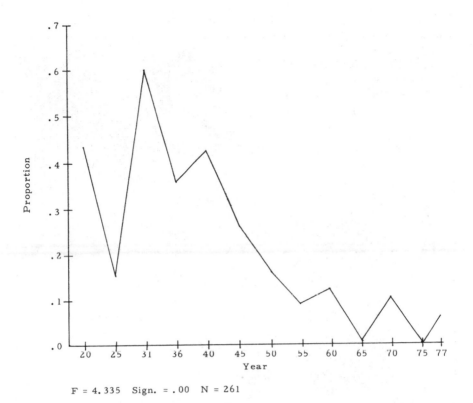

Figure 4.8. Proportion of Advertisements Depicting Child-care by
Mothers, by Year.

There was another change in the depiction of mothers in advertising. Although mothers, as compared to fathers, have always been
portrayed as more involved in the physical care aspects of parenthood such as feeding, bathing, and dressing, the play aspects of child-
care become more prevalent for mothers over time. For instance,
mothers are shown in the following recreational activities with their
children: traveling, picnicking, listening to the radio, watching television, and playing "board" games. This is consistent with Wolfenstein's (1952) analysis of popular child-rearing manuals and what she
called the emergence of a "fun morality" in child-rearing.

Titus (1976, p. 527), in her analysis of family photo albums,
found a distinction between mothers exhibiting physical care of
children and fathers being involved in play. Mothers were much more

Illustration 4.1.   Mother's Role in Physical Care of Children.

(From January 29, 1940 issue of *Life*. Reproduced with permission of Johnson & Johnson Company.)

likely than fathers, for example, to have been photographed feeding the baby. According to Nye's (1976, p. 51) analysis, the normative expectations expressed by his respondents support this idea that mothers are considered more responsible for the physical care as-

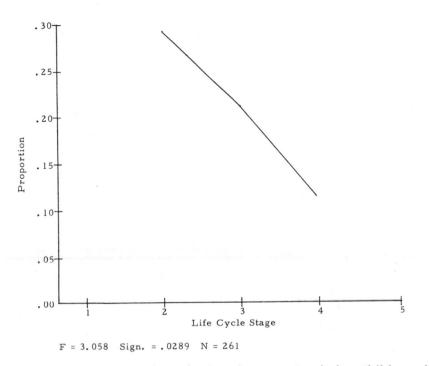

F = 3.058   Sign. = .0289   N = 261

Figure 4.9.   Proportion of Advertisements Depicting Child-care by
Mothers, by Family Life Cycle.

pects of parenthood. Consistent with these normative expectations,
Nye's respondents reported that mothers were, in fact, more likely
than fathers to carry out the physical aspects of child-care.

The offspring's sex made no difference in the likelihood of the
mother engaging in child-care. All children, regardless of sex, require
such physical care services as feeding, dressing, etc. However, the
number of female children was found to have an inverse effect on the
mother's likelihood of being portrayed in child-care (Table A.7). As
will be discussed later, there was greater likelihood of the older female child being portrayed as helping mother with child-care, which
explains this relationship.

When looking at changes in the portrayal of the mother's role in
child-care over the family life cycle, one finds a significant decrease
in emphasis (as seen in Figure 4.9). Analysis of variance indicated that
this relationship between the mother's role in child-care and family
life cycle remained the same over the time period 1920 to 1978 (2-
way interaction, F = 1.510, p = .07). No doubt this is a result of the

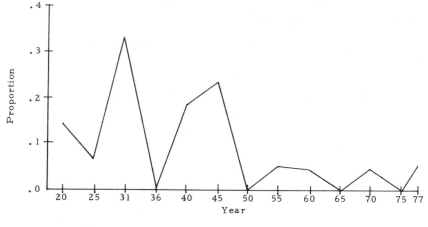

F = 1.763   Sign. = .05   N = 200

Figure 4.10.   Proportion of Advertisements Depicting Child-care by Fathers, by Year.

lessening need of physical care for children as they grow older. Since it is the physical care aspects in which mothers have predominated, it is not surprising to see this decrease over the family life cycle; and it is precisely older children with whom mothers are more likely to be depicted playing. In other words, mothers are more likely to be involved in the play aspects of child-care later in the family life cycle.

FATHERS

Child-care

As alluded to several times in the discussion of the mother's role, fathers are more likely to be depicted in the "play" aspects of child-care. Looking at the time period since 1920, the *overall* portrayal of fathers engaged in child-care has been significantly deemphasized, with a peak having occurred in 1931 during the Depression (Figure 4.10)—also the high point for mothers involved in these activities. Assuming that advertisements reflect family life values, it seems evident that caring for other family members was an important issue at a time when people had little else to count on.

Child-care activities for fathers, specifically in 1931, did not differ from other years. Essentially, these activities were the "play" aspects of child-care, with the exception of fathers helping children with

Illustration 4.2.   Father's Role in Play Aspects of Child-care.

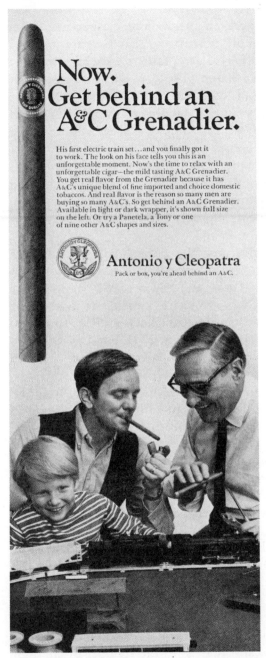

(From March 13, 1970 issue of *Life*. Reproduced with permission of the American Cigar Company.)

homework, where we see a reflection of the popular belief that men exceed women intellectually.

In order to explain the fathers' emphasis on play aspects of child-care, one must go beyond simply postulating that because mothers were given responsibility for physical care, fathers were allocated the "leftover" recreational duties. Slater (1961, p. 305) suggests that fathers have become pals to their children. A strict father is dysfunctional in the twentieth century nuclear family arrangement in which the relationship between fathers and their children is potentially fragile due to the father's "absence from the home during most of the child's waking hours." It is precisely the fact that fatherhood has been defined largely in terms of providing financially for the children (Maxwell 1976, p. 387) that explains in large part their lesser involvement in the physical care aspects of parenthood: fathers are simply not around.

The family life values concerning the father's role in child-care that are reflected in advertising are consistent with research concerning actual behavior of fathers. Parke and Sawin (1977, p. 368), for one, found that, although fathers are just as capable as mothers of physically caring for infants, they are less likely actually to do so. Likewise, Rendina and Dickerscheid (1977, p. 373) found that fathers are more involved in what they refer to as "social activities" than in the physical care of infants.

On a fairly consistent basis, advertisements since 1920 have depicted fathers about twice as likely to play with sons as opposed to daughters (Table A.8). This finding reaffirms Rendina and Dickerscheid's (1977, p. 376) finding that fathers of male infants were more involved than fathers of female infants in overall participation. Therefore, it is not that fathers simply play with male children because they find male recreational activities more agreeable; there appears to be a definite preference towards male offspring, even at the infant level.

The concept of fathers playing with infants raises the question of possible changes in the father's role in child-care over the family life cycle. According to advertisements, fathers do not significantly change their involvement in such activities over the life cycle (Tables A.9 and A.10). But, regardless of the family life cycle stage depicted or the time period, the number of children is related inversely to the father's involvement in child-care; that is, as the number of children increases, particularly the number of female children, child-care for fathers is less evident (Table A.7). Given the fact that the number of children increases over the family life cycle, one might assume that there is a contradiction between the lack of significant change in fathers' involvement in child-care over the family life cycle and the fact that such a depiction is inversely related to the number of children. The explanation is that the father's involvement in child-care is influenced by different factors at different stages of the family life cycle. In the early stages when children require more physical care, fathers are less likely to be portrayed. In the later stages, when the play aspects are stressed, the father's involvement is inversely affected by the increasing number of children. The overall pattern is an apparent lack of significant change in the father's involvement in child-care.

SIBLINGS–OFFSPRING–GRANDCHILDREN

The family positions of siblings, offspring, and grandchildren have been combined because their roles are essentially the same, at least in advertisements.

Brothers–sons–grandsons

In their positions as brothers, sons, and grandsons, male family members are depicted overwhelmingly in recreational activities. The cultural values reflected in advertising support the contention that this is the "century of the child." As Aries (1962) points out, the concept of childhood has been an emerging one, with the family becoming increasingly child-centered. The notion of children as something other than miniature adults is a relatively recent development, and the emphasis on depicting young brothers, sons, and grandsons in play activities illustrates this notion of childhood as a distinct stage in the life cycle with expected behaviors unique to it.

This emphasis on recreation for male siblings, offspring, and grandchildren has been prevalent over the entire period since 1920 and, in fact, has become increasingly the case, although not significantly (Tables A.11 and A.12). There has been a consistent trend over the family life cycle as well (Tables A.13 and A.14).

With respect to the actual recreational activities engaged in by these young male family members, there has not been any substantial change since 1920. Some of the more popular activities were reading, camping, biking, television viewing, and playing with model trains.

Sisters~daughters~granddaughters

The picture is essentially the same for sisters, daughters, and granddaughters; they are primarily depicted in recreational activities, and this portrayal has not changed significantly since 1920 or over the family life cycle (Tables A.15, A.16, A.17, and A.18).

However, when comparing the types of recreational activities of female children with those of male children, one finds some differences, although not as much as one might expect given recent complaints about sex role stereotyping in advertising. Both male and female children are depicted in such activities as camping, reading, traveling, picnicking, and playing tennis. The reason for this nonsexist depiction is that brothers and sisters often are shown jointly participating in these activities. As Irish (1964, p. 282) points out, "brothers and sisters spend many hours together and share a wide range of activities." At the same time, however, there was a certain amount of sex role stereotyping: girls playing with dolls and boys playing with trains. Nonetheless, it was the similarity in recreational activities of male and female children, rather than the differences, that stood out.

Although recreation was the major activity in ads featuring children of both sexes, female children were more likely than males to be depicted in household task performance and child-care. Female children were not often depicted in these specific roles (ten advertisements for household tasks and two for child-care), but these figures were higher than for the male counterparts (seven for household tasks and zero for child-care). The activities themselves were quite sex steroryped, with girls doing such jobs as cooking and cleaning, while boys were involved in the "heavy work" such as yard detail and carrying firewood.

In terms of family life cycle changes in the depiction of female children doing housework, significantly, nine of the ten advertisements portray families at the fourth stage (Figure 4.11). This is consistent with Powell's (1963, p. 234) finding that household tasks are often passed on to adolescent children rather than husbands.

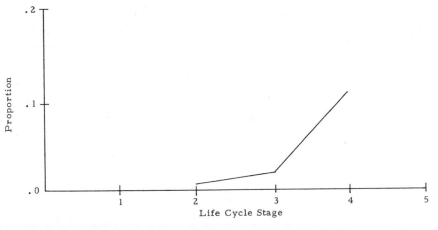

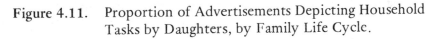

F = 7.476   Sign. = .0007   N = 218

Figure 4.11.   Proportion of Advertisements Depicting Household
Tasks by Daughters, by Family Life Cycle.

GRANDPARENTS

One of the desired contributions of the present study was an analysis of the cultural values since 1920 concerning the family position
of the grandparent. As Neugarten and Weinstein (1964, p. 199) point
out:

> Despite the proliferation of the investigations regarding the relations
> between generations and the position of the aged within the family,
> surprisingly little attention has been paid directly to the role of grand-
> parent.

Unfortunately, the present study can shed little light on this issue
except to say that grandparents have not been considered important
family members, at least in advertisements since 1920. Of the advertisements analyzed, only 17 grandmothers and nine grandfathers
were depicted. Possibly the emergence of the modified-extended
family explains part of the absence of grandparents, and yet, as
Adams (1968) contends, interaction with extended kin continues to
be an important factor of family life. In addition, as Robertson

(1976, p. 140) found, grandparents are still seen by grandchildren as important sources of gifts, family history, and emotional gratification. Clavan (1978, p. 351) sheds some light on this issue when she points out that there are no normative rights and obligations attached to the role of grandparent. It may be the difference of opinion as to what this role entails that makes it difficult to depict in advertising.

A closer look at the activities of grandparents will provide further explanation as to why they appear so infrequently. Essentially both grandmothers (11 out of 17 cases) and grandfathers (six out of nine cases) are depicted playing with their grandchildren. This is consistent with the research of Robertson (1977, p. 171), who found that the three activities in which grandmothers were engaged most frequently were baby-sitting, visiting, and playing with grandchildren. Neugarten and Weinstein (1964, p. 199) account for this emphasis on play as a result of the fact that grandparents in our culture are removed from family authority positions. In fact, Robertson (1977, p. 171) suggests grandmothers may fear that parents view too much interaction with grandchildren as meddlesome, intrusive, or inappropriate. For this reason alone, advertisers may deliberately avoid the grandparent model. Finally, Clavan (1978, p. 353) offers additional explanation of this low frequency by calling attention to the fact that the middle class is less marked by "functional centrality," namely, the degree to which extended kin are integrated into everyday family life. Since the advertisements used in the present study reflect middle-class values, one would expect less attention paid to grandparents because of their lesser "functional centrality."

Even though grandparents were seldom portrayed, one would have expected them to appear more frequently earlier in the century. Grandfathers were portrayed most often in 1925 (three times), but, contrary to this expectation, grandmothers were depicted most frequently (six times) in 1977. What this indicates about the importance of grandmothers and grandfathers since 1920 is difficult to say, given such a small data set.

In concurrence with Robertson's (1977, p. 173) suggestion that the role of grandmothers (and no doubt grandfathers as well) changes with the age of the child, the present analysis indicates that grandparents are more likely (ten out of 17 cases) to be depicted interacting with families at the second stage of the family life cycle, when all children are under six years of age. More than likely, as families progress through the family life cycle, the number of grandparents decreases due to death. Furthermore, young grandchildren whom they once baby-sat for and played with have grown and now have interests of their own.

SUMMARY

Since 1920, the portrayal of wives in magazine advertising has evidenced a change in terms of an increased emphasis on household task performance and recreation. The depiction of their role in economic provision and therapeutics has remained essentially the same. In terms of the family life cycle, there have been no significant changes in the wives' involvement in housework, recreation, or economic provision. However, the presence of children at family life cycle stages two, three, and four is associated with a decrease in the wives' involvement in therapeutic activities toward their husbands.

In spite of the fact that economic provision for husbands has been emphasized more strongly during some time periods than others (particularly during times of economic stress), it has always received more emphasis than the wives' responsibility for this role. Overall, one would have to conclude that the cultural values continue to support the idea that economic provision is an integral part of the husband's role; however, it is not all work and no play. Recreation has been increasingly emphasized since 1920, and both this role and economic provision have been stressed throughout the family life cycle. On the other hand, household task performance and therapeutics have received little attention as aspects of the husband's role, at least as depicted in magazine advertising.

From a general perspective, mothers are still more likely to be depicted in the physical care aspects of parenthood, while fathers are more likely to be involved in the play aspects (see Illustrations 4.1 and 4.2). The mother's involvement in child-care did show a decrease; however, it does not seem to have decreased because of any compensating increase in the father's involvement.

The decreasing emphasis on child-care for fathers since 1920 brings into question the emergence of fatherhood that one hears so much about lately. However, it is possible that this emergence is too recent to have been reflected in magazine advertisements. There were no significant changes in the portrayal of fathers engaged in child-care over the family life cycle, but mothers were portrayed decreasingly in the physical care aspects and increasingly in the play aspects over the family life cycle.

When it comes to the roles of siblings, offspring, and grandchildren, one thing is very clear: since at least 1920, their roles have overwhelmingly involved recreation. In addition, the family life cycle stage depicted made little difference. This has truly been at least the "half-century" of the child.

Finally, the role of grandparents received surprisingly little attention, even during the earlier time periods. Those advertisements that did include grandparents portrayed them as involved primarily in child-care, particularly families at stage two, where all children are under six years of age.

In conclusion, when one takes a look at the changes in the depiction of family roles in magazine advertising since 1920, the fact emerges that certain roles have changed somewhat while others have remained essentially the same. Change, then, in the cultural values concerning family roles is not a unidimensional concept. In addition, some of these changes have been more dramatic for families at particular stages of the family life cycle. However, when one looks at the "three pillars" of family roles—economic provision, household task performance, and child-care—the changes do not suggest any dramatic shift toward a more egalitarian family role structure. This is not surprising, since it is the familial aspect of sex roles that seems to change the slowest (Roper and LaBeff 1977, p. 118) and that males and females seem to agree upon the most (Osmond and Martin 1975, p. 744).

CHAPTER **V**

Family Companionship

In the present study, companionship is defined as activities that family members share jointly. Much of the previous research has limited this definition to leisure activities; however, this chapter will also consider other aspects of family life that can be shared. As Edgell (1972, p. 457) points out:

> When companionship is defined solely in terms of shared leisure, it is not surprising to find that... companionship declines after the courtship stage and notably after the birth of the first child.

By extending the potential range of activities, one might find that companionship in certain aspects of family life actually increases over the family life cycle or that it essentially remains the same. As in the preceding chapter, all findings refer to changes in the images of family life in magazine advertisements.[1]

HUSBAND–FATHER/WIFE–MOTHER COMPANIONSHIP

Household tasks

As discussed in the preceding chapter, household tasks have been depicted as primarily the wife's responsibility. However, other family members, in particular husbands, have been portrayed as sharing in

---

[1] Tables discussed in this chapter can be found in Appendix B.

these activities. Husbands and wives have sometimes been shown sharing the cooking, cleaning, and, particularly, the "maintenance" aspects of housework such as painting. This sharing of household tasks by husbands and wives increased significantly since 1920, indicating a change in the cultural norms towards a more companionate form of marriage, at least in terms of household task performance (Figure 5.1).

Nevertheless, as seen in Figure 5.2, a significant decline exists in this sharing over the family life cycle. Those advertisements that depicted housework were more likely to portray husband-wife companionship for families at the earlier stages. Analysis of variance showed no significant interaction effect, indicating that this relationship held for all years under investigation (2-way interactions, $F = .471$, $p = .944$).

In order to explain the decrease in husband-wife sharing of housework over the family life cycle, it is helpful to look at the effect that the number of children has on the relationship. As the number of children increases, regardless of their sex, husband-wife companionship in housework decreases (Table B.1). Although children are not

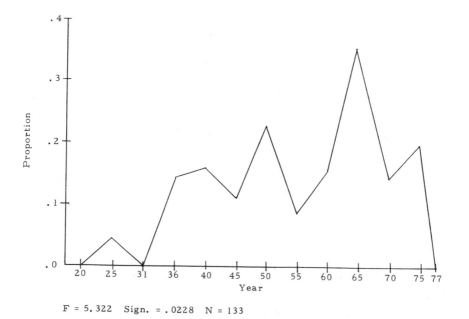

$F = 5.322$ Sign. $= .0228$ N = 133

Figure 5.1.   Proportion of Advertisements Depicting Husband-Wife Companionship in Household Tasks by Year.

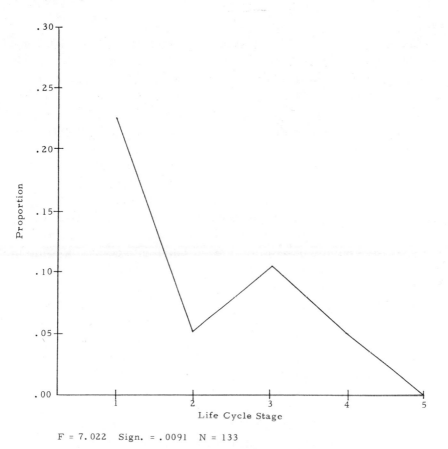

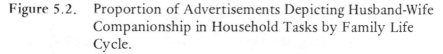

F = 7.022   Sign. = .0091   N = 133

Figure 5.2. Proportion of Advertisements Depicting Husband-Wife Companionship in Household Tasks by Family Life Cycle.

portrayed frequently as sharing household tasks with their parents, it seems that the very presence of children decreases the likelihood of husbands and wives sharing this activity. This could be a reflection of the fact that in families with children, particularly older children, they serve as a new batch of potential "recruits" to help the wife with what is essentially considered her responsibility. Another possible explanation is that the overall egalitarian pattern, more common among preparental couples, is gradually replaced by a more differentiated division of labor between husband and wife when children have become part of the family, regardless of whether the children share in household tasks or not.

Child-care

Magazine advertising has painted a picture of both mothers and fathers being responsible for child-care, albeit in terms of different activities. Mothers have been depicted as primarily responsible for the physical care aspects of parenthood, while fathers have been depicted as primarily involved in the play aspects. But what of shared child-care activities? Has there been any change in husband-wife companionship in child-care since 1920?

The evidence from the present study indicates that no significant change took place in husband-wife companionship in child-care activities (Table B.2). The pattern, however, is interesting. One of the high points occurred in 1936 during the Depression. Possibly an emphasis on family cooperation during this stressful time explains the increase. One might assume that husband-wife companionship in child-care would have been high during the baby boom years between 1945 and 1955. However, although not significantly lower than other years analyzed, the years 1945, 1950, and 1955 were among those that least emphasized husband-wife sharing of child-care. After the baby boom years there was increased emphasis; most of these subsequent years were among those that most emphasized husband-wife companionship in child-care.

It may be that the increased emphasis only appears when the children of the baby boom have grown older. This explanation is supported by the fact that most of the advertisements portraying husband-wife companionship in child-care involved the play aspects of parenting. That is, when sharing of this responsibility was depicted, it usually showed mother and father playing with the children rather than physically caring for them. It is this emphasis on the play aspects that may explain the lower emphasis during the baby boom years. When the children are young and require more physical care, mothers and fathers are less likely to share in child-care activities. However, as a majority of the children of the baby boom reached the point (around the beginning of the 1960s) where play made up a larger portion of parents' involvement in child-care, mothers and fathers were increasingly portrayed as sharing in this activity.

Further support for this explanation is provided by analysis of variance results. When one looks at the changes in mother-father companionship in the play aspects of child-care since 1920, there is a significant interaction effect ($F = 1.886$, $p = .009$) with family life cycle. The increase is particularly noticeable for the stages of the family life cycle when the children are older, stages four and five (Table B.3). Stone's (1963, p. 85) results showing that adolescents, regardless of their age, wish to share recreational activities with their families lends support to this finding.

Recreation

This aspect of husband-wife companionship has received the most attention in research literature. Blood and Wolfe (1960, p. 150), for example, contend that companionship has emerged as the most valued aspect of marriage, their measure being basically an index of shared leisure activities; however, their cross-sectional data can neither support nor refute such a contention.

Blood and Wolfe's (1960, p. 147) view is supported by magazine advertisements. In Figure 5.3, the longitudinal analysis indicates that advertisements since 1920 have increasingly emphasized shared recreational activities between husbands and wives. This significant increase was fairly consistent, except for a dramatic decline in 1931

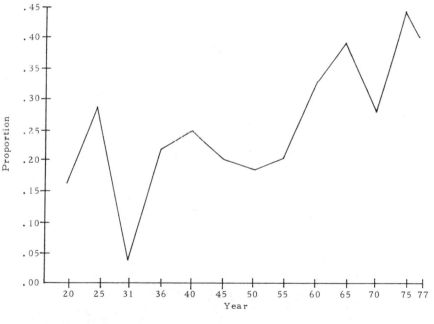

F = 9.664   Sign. = .002   N = 418

Figure 5.3.   Proportion of Advertisements Depicting Husband-Wife Companionship in Recreation by Year.

during the Depression, followed by a gradual increase until the war years, followed again by a slight decline. After 1945 the increased emphasis on husband-wife companionship in recreation is fairly consistent. This increase over time is due in part to women becoming more involved in athletic forms of recreation such as camping, tennis, and skiing. Therefore, there is a greater range of recreational activities that have the potential to be shared by spouses.

The fact that "the combination of relatively late marriage, short life expectancy, and high fertility rarely allowed for an 'empty nest' stage" in the nineteenth century (Hareven 1976, p. 17), also explains in part this emergence of shared recreation between husbands and wives. Put simply, husbands and wives have more years to devote to such activities after the "child-launching" stage.

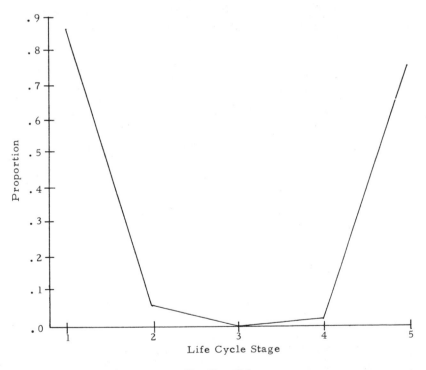

F = 345.496   Sign. = .00   N = 418

Figure 5.4.   Proportions of Advertisements Depicting Husband-Wife Companionship in Recreation by Family Life Cycle.

Analysis of variance indicated a significant interaction effect (F = 4.124, p = .000) between family life cycle and the passage of time. The increased emphasis on husband-wife shared recreation was most noted among families at the preparental and postparental stages of the family life cycle (Figure 5.4). As Burr (1970, p. 29) points out, various aspects of marital satisfaction are affected differently by passage through the family life cycle. Specifically, the results of the present study parallel Burr's (1970) finding that satisfaction with husband-wife companionship in recreation tends to be curvilinear; that is, husbands and wives not only report greater satisfaction with shared recreation during the preparental and postparental stages, but the cultural values reflected in magazine advertising suggest that this is an integral part of conjugal relationships at these stages of the family life cycle.

The present findings are contrary to Orthner's (1975) analysis, which showed that "joint leisure activities" decreased over the family life cycle and did not show a curvilinear relationship. This discrepancy may be explained by several factors.

First, Orthner (1975) was dealing with actual behavior, and the present study deals with cultural values. In addition, there are differences in the measurement of several variables in the two studies. For instance, Orthner (1975) differentiated between joint and parallel leisure activities, whereas these two types of shared leisure were combined in the present study. Orthner (1975, p. 93) defines the two concepts as follows:

> *Joint activities* require a high degree of interaction for successful completion of the activity and tend to open communication and encourage role interchange.
> *Parallel activities* are little more than individual activities in group settings and a minimum of interaction is allowed among the participants.

As such, he found that joint leisure activities decreased over the family life cycle, while parallel leisure activities remained about the same. By combining these two types in the present study, the decrease in joint activities may be masked by the relative stability of parallel activities.

Possibly an even more important issue in explaining the discrepant findings is the fact that Orthner's (1975, p. 95) measure of the family life cycle, or what he refers to as the "marital career," does not control for the number of children. It is quite possible that even during the first and last stages of the "marital career," children were included. This was not the case in the present study; therefore, the curvilinear effects attributable to the presence or absence of children are more evident.

Rollins and Cannon's (1974, p. 281) explanation of the curvilinear relationship between marital satisfaction and family life cycle would apply also to the curvilinear relationship between the depiction of husband-wife companionship in recreation and family life cycle.[2] Their interpretation, based on role theory, states that:

> It seems reasonable that it would be during periods of time when the number of intensity of roles of an individual are greatest that role conflict, role incompatability, and the amount of activity that is normatively prescribed in a person's life would be at a maximum. These data along with role theory suggest that role strain would be greatest and marital satisfaction would be least at the middle stages of the family life cycle and role strain would be least and marital satisfaction greatest at both ends of the family life cycle.

It seems likely that the increased family responsibilities that occur when children become part of the family might well lead to a role overload situation, thus leaving less time available for shared husband-wife recreation. Further support for this position is supplied by the fact that, in the present study, as the number of children increased, regardless of their sex, emphasis on husband-wife companionship in recreation decreased.

PARENT–CHILD COMPANIONSHIP IN RECREATION

The magazine advertisements strongly reflected the cultural value that "the family that plays together stays together." In fact, in terms

---

[2] Cautionary arguments concerning the curvilinear relationship between family life cycle and marital satisfaction have been raised by Spanier, Lewis, and Cole (1975), Miller (1975), and Schram (1979). Schram (1979) discusses several confounding variables that may be involved in producing this curvilinear relationship. For example, the fact that dissatisfied couples are likely to be selected out through divorce before reaching later stages of the family life cycle needs to be taken into account.

of companionship, parents are depicted as sharing little with their children other than recreation. Occasionally, a child is shown sharing in housework or child-care, but this is the rare exception.

According to Nye (1976, p. 132), there has been "little research that focuses on the interaction patterns associated with family recreation," and yet it is apparently an important aspect of family life. Nye (1976, p. 137) found that a large proportion of spouses agreed that responsibility to provide for family recreation ought to be either the husband's, the wife's, or a joint responsibility. In other words, which family member organizes family recreation is less important

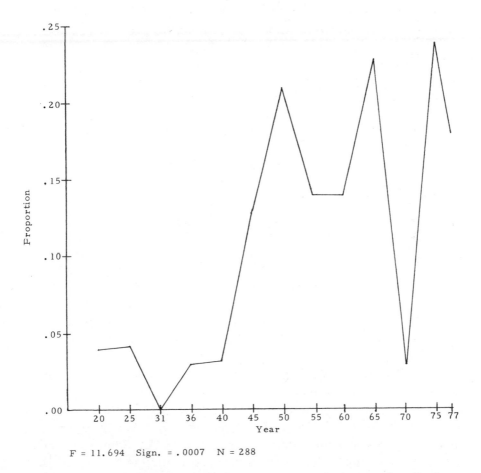

F = 11.694   Sign. = .0007   N = 288

Figure 5.5.   Proportion of Advertisements Depicting Mother-Father-Son-Daughter Companionship in Recreation by Year.

than the fact that someone does it. The overabundance (80 percent) of advertisements depicting family members sharing recreational activities is also evidence of its importance to family life.

Has the importance of family companionship in recreation always been with us? Orthner (1975, p. 91) claims that earlier studies (Parsons and Bales 1955) supporting a decline in the recreational function of the family have been supplanted by studies suggesting the importance of such activities in family life (Hobart 1963, Edwards 1967, Dumazedier 1967, Kelly 1972). It is not possible that all these studies were in fact tapping the emergence of the recreational role to which Nye (1976) alludes? As Nye (1976, p. 131) observes, "longer paid vacations, shorter work weeks, and more three-day weekends provide increased time for recreational activities."

Since it relies on longitudinal data, the present analysis has an advantage over Nye's (1976) study in that it can more adequately address the issue of whether or not companionship in recreation has emerged as a more important aspect of family life. When one studies these activities in magazine advertising, one finds that there has been a significant increase in emphasis on shared recreation for the entire nuclear family unit (Figure 5.5).

However, this significant increase in emphasis on shared family recreation has not been the same for all family life cycle stages. There is a significant interaction effect ($F = 1.886$, $p = .009$) between the historical passage of time and the family life cycle, with families at stage three showing that most dramatic increase since 1920. This is due to the fact that the relationship between companionship in recreation and the family life cycle is significantly curvilinear (Figure 5.6). Little shared recreation occurred between parents and children at stage two, no doubt because the range of possible recreational activities is more limited relative to those available to older children and their parents. At stage four there was a decrease in shared recreation, though nowhere near the low level of families at stage two. Possibly, the children in families at stage four are thought to have many more outside interests of their own.

This notion of "recreational activities of their own" is particularly noticeable when one looks at the sharing of such activities between parents and their adult children (stage five). The predominant recreational activity that parents were portrayed as sharing with their adult

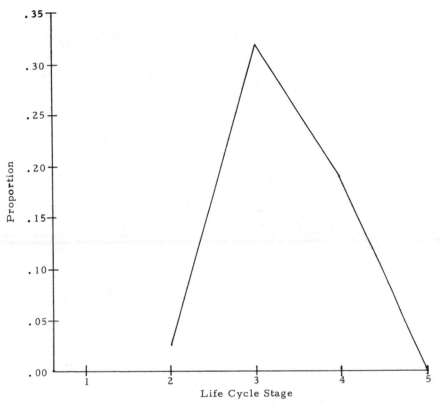

F = 19.634   Sign. = .00   N = 288

Figure 5.6.   Proportion of Advertisements Depicting Mother-Father-Son-Daughter Companionship in Recreation by Family Life Cycle.

children was visiting, particularly during holiday seasons. Thus, advertisements show extended families happily gathered around the Thanksgiving turkey or birthday cake. Several studies (Nimkoff 1961, Adams 1968, Ward 1978) support the notion that a major form of shared recreation between parents and adult children is what Adams (1968) refers to in his analysis of urban kinship patterns as "ritual reunions."

In addition, as the family moves through the life cycle, there is an increase in the number of children portrayed. This increase in children allows for more of a potential shift away from parent-child companionship in recreation to sibling companionship in recreation.[3]

SIBLINGS COMPANIONSHIP IN RECREATION

Is there a tendency to depict particular sexed siblings sharing recreation? The evidence indicates that, overall, brothers prefer sharing leisure activities with brothers and sisters with sisters.

Looking at Figure 5.7, it is evident that *cross-sexed* sibling companionship in recreation has become significantly less desirable since 1920. A significant curvilinear relationship was found between brother-sister companionship in recreation and the family life cycle (see Figure 5.8), with those families at stage three emphasizing shared recreation the most. However, the negative relationship between brother-sister companionship in recreation over time was found for all stages of the family life cycle (2-way interactions, $F = .833$, $p = .693$).

An analysis of the older siblings' sex in these situations indicated that males were more likely to be the older sibling. What we may be seeing here is an emphasis on the big-brother, little-sister syndrome, where the older sibling is looked upon as a source of companionship as well as protection. This is not to suggest that brothers and sisters at either stages two or four cannot differ in age, but rather that the distinguishing characteristic between siblings at stage three is more a matter of one child having entered school (a major rite of passage) and the other not having done so. In other words, it is the fact that one sibling is somehow more "worldly" than the other and thus is looked up to that may explain the greater likelihood of portraying cross-sexed companionship in recreation at this stage of the family life cycle.

It may well be the ever-increasing sex differentiated activities of male and female siblings that explains the decrease in cross-sexed

---

[3] As mentioned in the previous chapter concerning mothers' and fathers' roles in child-care, it was found that fathers were about twice as likely to be shown playing (a form of child-care) with sons as opposed to daughters. Mothers, on the other hand, were just as likely to be found playing with children of either sex.

sibling companionship in recreation at stage four. The fact that often one of the children portrayed at stage two is still an infant may explain the almost identical decrease that occurs for cross-sexed siblings at stage two; the possibility of shared recreation is relatively limited.

SUMMARY

The present results support the contention that companionship has emerged as a more important aspect of family life. This increase

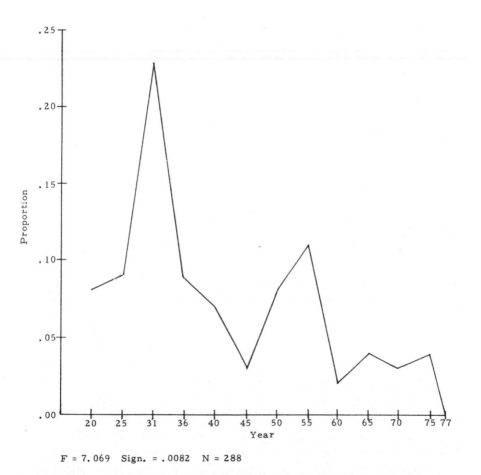

F = 7.069   Sign. = .0082   N = 288

Figure 5.7.   Proportion of Advertisements Depicting Brother-Sister Companionship in Recreation by Year.

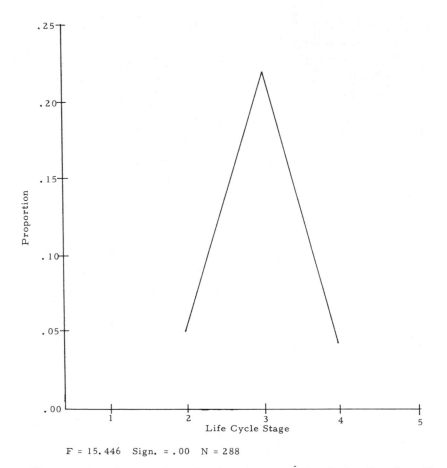

F = 15.446   Sign. = .00   N = 288

Figure 5.8.   Proportion of Advertisements Depicting Brother-Sister
Companionship in Recreation by Family Life Cycle.

in the importance of companionship among family members was reflected in magazine advertisements (see Illustrations 5.1 and 5.2).

In terms of the husband-wife relationship, an increased emphasis
was placed on companionship in household task performance since
1920, particularly for families at the earlier stages of the life cycle.
Companionship in the "play" aspects of child-care was also found to
increase over time, especially for families at stages three and four.
Companionship in recreation also increased since 1920, most notice-
ably during the preparental and postparental stages.

Illustration 5.1.   Low Degree of Family Companionship in House-
                          hold Tasks.

(From April 15, 1940 issue of *Life*. Reproduced with permission of Compton
Advertising Incorporated.)

Illustration 5.2. High Degree of Family Companionship in Household Tasks.

"It's a Maytag...I didn't need any other reason to get a Maytag Dishwasher," writes Mrs. Di Mango.

"My Maytag clothes washer is going on 11, and it's never needed a repair. How do you stay in business when your appliances last so long?"

THE MAYTAG COMPANY, NEWTON, IOWA. WASHERS, DRYERS, PORTABLE WASHERS AND DRYERS, DISHWASHERS, DISPOSERS.

"Would you believe I used to have a dishwasher I only used 12 times in 20 years?" writes Mrs. Mafalda Di Mango of Brooklyn, New York. "I had to rinse and practically wash all my dishes before putting them in the machine. And then I sometimes had to wash them over again."

"What a change, now that I have a Maytag Dishwasher. It saves me all kinds of time and gets dishes as clean as I like."

Know why you're so pleased with your Maytag, Mrs. Di Mango? Maytag's exclusive Micro-Mesh™ Filter keeps the water cleaner. And Maytag has a full-size spray arm on top, as well as one below, for extra cleaning power! So your dishes get clean without pre-rinsing.

Giant capacity is another fine Maytag convenience. It's the only dishwasher that takes 10-inch plates in both racks.

See Maytag Built-In and Portable Dishwashers —and also Maytag Food Waste Disposers—at your Maytag Dealer's now. He's in the Yellow Pages.

We don't say that Mrs. Di Mango's dishwasher will equal the record of her washer. But dependability is what we try to build into every Maytag. No matter what job it's made for.

MAYTAG
THE DEPENDABILITY PEOPLE

Joanne, 15½; Mrs. Di Mango; Patricia, 17.

Mail coupon for beautifully illustrated booklet.
The Maytag Company
Dept. LI-11, Newton, Iowa 50208
I enclose 10¢. Send me your illustrated booklet that gives full details about dependable Maytag Built-In and Portable Dishwashers, and Maytag Food Waste Disposers, too.
I'm thinking of (check one):
☐ Replacing ☐ Remodeling ☐ Building

Name_____
Address_____
City_____
State_____ Zip_____

(From November 13, 1970 issue of *Life*. Reproduced with permission of The Maytag Company.)

With regard to parent-child companionship, recreation was the activity overwhelmingly emphasized. The slogan "the family which prays together, stays together," can be rephrased for magazine advertising as the family that plays together, stays together. In fact, this has been increasingly emphasized since 1920, particularly for families at stage three of the family life cycle.

Finally, same-sexed sibling companionship in recreation was found to be the preferred pattern; this factor has not changed significantly since 1920 or over the family life cycle. Further, cross-sexed sibling companionship in recreation was found to have become increasingly less popular over time.

In conclusion, the cultural values reflected in magazine advertising suggest that family companionship has become increasingly important, particularly companionship in recreational activities. As Orthner (1975, p. 101) says:

> The ability of leisure to influence the family may be increasing and if the family is moving toward companionship as a source of marital solidarity, then the leisure factor is of critical importance.

CHAPTER **VI**

Family Intimacy

Although we tend to take intimacy between family members for granted, Shorter (1975) and others assert to its relatively recent origin as a characteristic of family life. Burgess, Locke, and Thomes (1945) note how intimacy has become increasingly characteristic of family relationships in their reference to the family evolving from institution to companionship.

> The point of their discussion is that increasingly family behavior has become a function of "mutual affection and consensus of its members" rather than "mores, public opinion, and law." (Kerckhoff 1972, p. 22).

Previous literature on family intimacy suffers from a lack of conceptual clarity, particularly with respect to the terms companionship and intimacy, which have often been used interchangeably. This would be less of a problem if at least the concepts (whatever one chooses to call them) were operationalized in a consistent fashion. Unfortunately, some of the measurement techniques used tend to combine aspects of both companionship and intimacy under the same summary score and then refer to it as an index of either companionship or intimacy.[1]

---

[1] See Straus and Brown (1978) for a source of techniques that measure family intimacy and companionship. In particular, J.L. Hawkins' "Marital Companionship Scale" and R.G. Tharp's "Marriage Role Dimensions" seem to suffer from this problem.

73

What exactly is family intimacy and how does it differ from companionship? Using Webster's *New Collegiate Dictionary* (1975) as a source, this author refers to companionship as the act of "keeping company or associating with" another in some shared activity. Intimacy, on the other hand, refers to the degree of "closeness, contact, or familiarity" between two people regardless of whether or not they are sharing an activity. Consequently, the fact that family members are sharing activities does not necessarily imply that they are on intimate terms with each other; it does not necessitate a strong bond between them, a mutual deep caring, or mutual self-disclosures, all of which are indicators of intimacy.

In the present analysis, these indicators were unavailable, so physical distance between family members in the advertisements was used as a measurement of family intimacy.[2] To illustrate the difference between companionship and intimacy, and to illustrate the use of physical distance as a measure of intimacy, the previously used example is offered again. Family members can share the activity of watching television together (companionship) either by sitting in separate chairs (less intimate) or by holding each other closely on the couch (more intimate). Likewise, family members can engage in separate activities—the husband reading and the wife writing letters (lack of companionship)—either by sitting in separate chairs (less intimate) or by sitting closely together on the couch (more intimate). Again, the results discussed in this chapter refer to family images in magazine advertising.[3]

HUSBAND–WIFE INTIMACY

Some researchers such as Smith (1973) suggest and provide evidence that, as a result of industrialization, males became less dependent on the necessity to inherit land from their fathers as a means of self-support. In addition, industrialization provided females with an increasing potential to support themselves. As a result of these alternative sources of monetary rewards, mate selection became based on

---

[2] See the discussion of Levinger and Gunner's (1967) "interpersonal grid" on page 24 for an explanation of such a measure of family intimacy.

[3] Tables discussed in this chapter can be found in Appendix C.

more romantic motives. Chudacoff and Hareven (1979) note that, contrary to the experience of nineteenth century households, most twentieth century families experience an "empty nest" stage where husband-wife intimacy takes on new importance. Furthermore, the expressive dimension of husband-wife relationships increased in importance as the state took over some of the instrumental functions previously delegated to the family unit.

The present findings are consistent with this notion of increased intimacy between husbands and wives. Figure 6.1 shows how husband-wife intimacy increased significantly in advertisements published between 1920 and 1978. Overall, there was a consistent increase, except for the period 1940 to 1955. One might readily attribute the initial decrease after 1940 to the fact that many husbands were overseas fighting in the Second World War; however, why the downward trend continues beyond 1945 is not readily apparent. One possibility that suggests itself is that somehow the baby boom is involved. The increased responsibilities for child-care might have a negative effect on husband-wife intimacy. It is possible that the cultural values reflected in magazine advertising during the period 1945 to

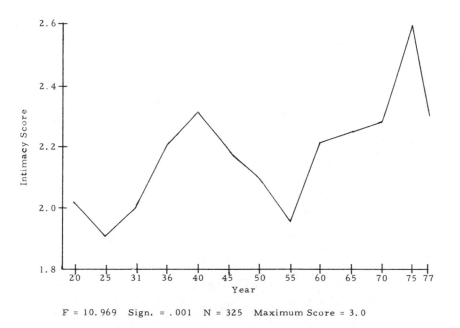

F = 10.969   Sign. = .001   N = 325   Maximum Score = 3.0

Figure 6.1.   Mean Husband-Wife Intimacy Score by Year.

1955 emphasized parent-child intimacy more than husband-wife intimacy.

Support for this position is provided by the analysis of husband-wife intimacy over the family life cycle. A significant curvilinear relationship was found between these two variables, with the preparental and postparental stages showing the highest levels of husband-wife intimacy (Figure 6.2). Although there was also a significant negative relationship between the number of children depicted and husband-wife intimacy, the age of the children appears to be a partial factor. Husband-wife intimacy is greater at stage four, when all the children are over six years of age, then at stage three, where preschool children might interfere with husband-wife intimacy.

The dramatic increase in the depiction of husband-wife intimacy at the postparental stage (even higher than the preparental stage) is

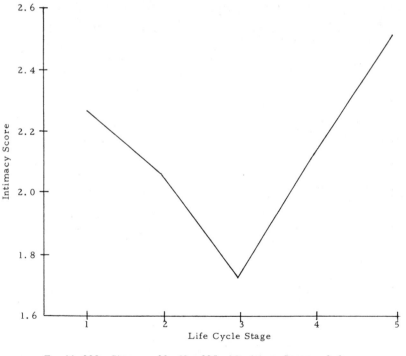

F = 11.999   Sign. = .00   N = 325   Maximum Score = 3.0

Figure 6.2.   Mean Husband-Wife Intimacy Score by Family Life Cycle.

consistent with Stinnett, Carter, and Montgomery's (1972, p. 666) analysis of senior citizens' perceptions of their marriages, in which "being able to express true feelings to each other" (an aspect of intimacy) was one of the most rewarding aspects of the respondents' marital relationships. Similar results were obtained by Lipman's (1961) research, "in which it was found that the expressive qualities...were seen by older couples as the most important things a couple could give each other in the latter years of marriage" (Stinnett, Carter, and Montgomery, 1972, p. 669).

Analysis of variance indicated that the increase in husband-wife intimacy since 1920 was found for families at all life cycle stages (2-way interactions, F = 1.177, p = .218) and was highest when these marital partners were sharing recreational activities.

In addition, husband-wife intimacy was relatively higher when they shared housework. This was generally the case since 1940, especially for families in the first three stages of the family life cycle. However, husband-wife intimacy was also relatively high when wives were shown doing housework alone, particularly during the fourth and fifth stages of the family life cycle. However, after 1965, high husband-wife intimacy was less likely to be seen in advertisements in which wives were doing housework alone; the message suggesting that sexual equality in the home put forth by the feminist movement may be reflected in advertising. That is, after 1965, husband-wife intimacy is higher when housework is *shared* by husbands and wives.

PARENT–CHILD INTIMACY

Given the fact that the portrayal of husband-wife intimacy has increased significantly since 1920, and given the fact that husband-wife intimacy decreased in the parental stages of the family life cycle, two questions come to mind. First, does the evolution of the family from institution to companionship (Burgess, Locke, and Thomes 1945) also apply to parent-child relationships? Second, how is parent-child intimacy affected by the family life cycle?

Parent–son intimacy

According to Martel's (1968, p. 51) analysis of American magazine fiction published between 1890 and 1955, there has been a shift away from cross-sexed attachments towards same-sexed attachments within the family:

> In 1890, close attachments are portrayed most frequently between mother-son, father-daughter, brother-sister and even uncles and nieces. By 1955, however, the shoe is on the other foot. . . .

Such a finding suggests that a similar pattern might apply to mother-son vs. father-son intimacy in advertisements. The present study found that neither mother-son intimacy nor father-son intimacy changed significantly since 1920 (Tables C.1 and C.2). However, the results, although not significant, do corroborate Martel's (1968) findings. A fairly consistent decrease in mother-son intimacy was found between 1936 and 1955, leveling off thereafter for the most part. At the same time, father-son intimacy remained essentially the same between 1931 and 1950, followed by a dramatic 15-year increase starting in 1955. More specifically, parent-son intimacy was highest when recreational activities were depicted in advertisements over the entire time period under investigation.

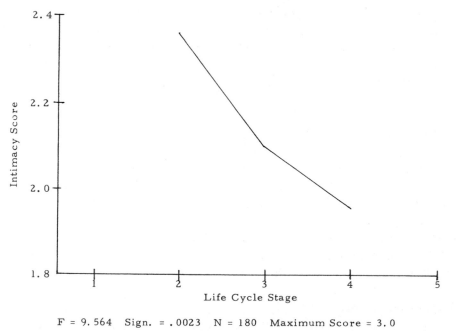

F = 9.564   Sign. = .0023   N = 180   Maximum Score = 3.0

Figure 6.3.   Mean Mother-Son Intimacy Score by Family Life Cycle.

A consistently significant decrease in both mother-son intimacy (Figure 6.3) and father-son intimacy (Figure 6.4) was found over the parental stages of the family life cycle. This is probably the result of the belief that as children grow older they extend their range of intimate relationships beyond that which exists in their parent-child relationship. In this case, sons are no longer exclusively intimate with parents, but now include siblings and friends into their circle of intimate contacts. Analysis of variance indicated that the decrease in mother-son intimacy (2-way interactions, F = .799, p = .734) and the decrease in father-son intimacy over the family life cycle (2-way interactions, F = 1.052, p = .410) held for all years under investigation. Even though parent-son intimacy was found to decrease over the family life cycle, these relationships were most likely to be intimate when the sharing of recreation was involved.

Due to the scarcity of advertisements depicting adult-child/parent interaction, it is difficult to come to any conclusions concerning intimacy between adult sons and parents. Of course, this lack of emphasis on parent-adult child interaction says something about the apparent

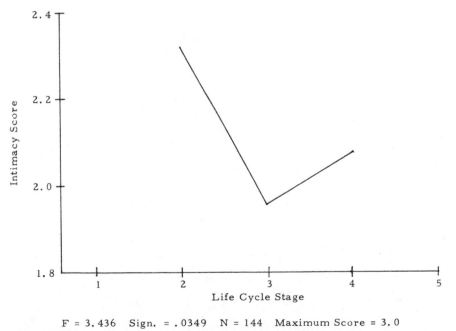

F = 3.436   Sign. = .0349   N = 144   Maximum Score = 3.0

Figure 6.4.   Mean Father-Son Intimacy Score by Family Life Cycle.

lack of importance of intimacy between adult sons and their parents.
However, such a conclusion is inconsistent with Cumming and Henry's
(1961) finding that people between 50 and 80 years of age felt closer
to their children than to siblings or spouses, and must, therefore, be
accepted cautiously.

Parent-daughter intimacy

There has been no significant change in mother-daughter intimacy in magazine advertising since 1920 (Table C.3). Similar to Martel's
(1968) findings, there was an increase in mother-daughter intimacy
between 1931 and 1950 and a general decrease in father-daughter
intimacy over the same time period. However, while father-son intimacy continued to increase after 1955, mother-daughter intimacy
decreased rather dramatically and fairly consistently after 1950.
Therefore, the shift toward same-sexed family attachments, which
Martel (1968) found in his analysis, seems to have continued only for

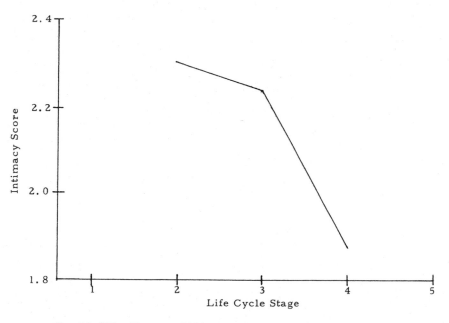

F = 13.627   Sign. = .0003   N = 190   Maximum Score = 3.0

Figure 6.5.   Mean Mother-Daughter Intimacy Score by Family Life
Cycle.

father-son intimacy and not for mother-daughter intimacy. As in the other cases, the most intimate depictions of mothers and daughters involved them sharing in recreational activities.

Figure 6.5 illustrates a significant decrease in mother-daughter intimacy throughout the parental stages of the family life cycle. Analysis of variance indicated a significant interaction effect ($F = 2.297$, $p = .001$) between family life cycle and historical time, with the decrease being greater after 1950. In spite of this decrease, mother-daughter intimacy was highest at all life cycle stages when recreation was being shared. Again, because of the dearth of advertisements portraying parent-adult child interaction, it is impossible to make any judgment as to whether the cultural values support an increase in mother-adult daughter intimacy. The research of Adams (1968) suggests that there might. He found that the mother-adult daughter is strong (in fact stronger than the mother-adult son bond) and that it is characterized by "role convergence," since both mother and daughter have the housewife role in common.

The results concerning father-daughter intimacy are most interesting, although not readily explainable. As can be seen in Figure 6.6, there is a significant ten-year cyclical pattern in father-daughter intimacy between 1920 and 1950, with 1920, 1931, and 1940 being high points.[4] After 1950, the cyclical pattern appears to continue, but now in a 15-year cycle. One wonders if somehow this pattern isn't a result of the taboo against fathers becoming "too close" to their daughters. Since the measurement of intimacy in the present analysis is based on physical distance, such a possibility seems plausible. The cultural values reflected in magazine advertisements alternate between fathers being intimate with and distant from their daughters. The pendulum swings away from intimacy when fathers are perceived as being portrayed as "too close." Again, recreational activities showed a high intimacy level in the father-daughter relationship despite the general pattern.

It would be interesting to compare father-daughter intimacy in magazine advertisements with advice in child-rearing manuals concerning the father-daughter relationship for the years 1920–1978.

---

[4] The significance of the cyclical pattern between 1920 and 1950 is supported by spectral analysis, which produced an auto correlation of -.51 for adjacent scores and an auto correlation of .83 for alternate scores.

Even more interesting would be to compare father-daughter intimacy in magazine advertisements with public concern over incest, possibly measured through an analysis of newspaper coverage.

Father-daughter intimacy was not found to change significantly over the family life cycle, and, again, the most intimate depictions involved shared recreation. The cyclical pattern over time was found to be consistent for families at all stages of the life cycle (2-way interactions, F = .740, p = .768).

Since parent-child intimacy was found to decrease significantly over the parental stages of the family life cycle, except for the father-daughter relationship (Table C.4)—and even this was in a decreasing direction—one might hypothesize that the portrayal of sibling inti-

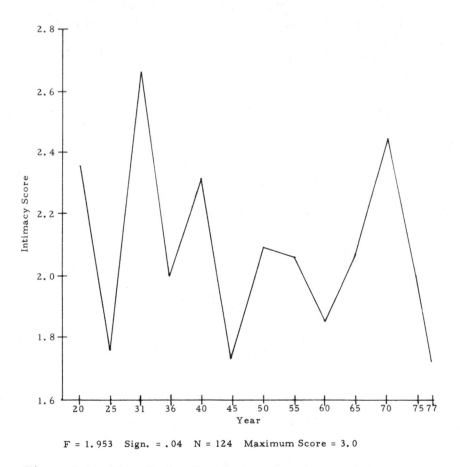

F = 1.953   Sign. = .04   N = 124   Maximum Score = 3.0

Figure 6.6.   Mean Father-Daughter Intimacy Score by Year.

macy might replace parent-child intimacy. Parent-child intimacy did decrease significantly as the number of children increased, regardless of their sex (Table C.5). However, as will be seen in the next section, changes in sibling intimacy over the family life cycle apparently do not play a significant part in explaining the decrease in parent-child intimacy.

SIBLING INTIMACY

Although research has found the parent-child relationship to be the closest, intimacy between siblings has been found to run a close second, particularly during certain stages of the family life cycle (Cumming and Schneider 1961, p. 499). Three questions concerning sibling intimacy were dealt with in the present study. First, have certain sibling combinations been portrayed as being more intimate than others? Second, has the importance of sibling intimacy always been with us? Finally, do values concerning sibling intimacy change over the family life cycle?

Several studies have found that the sister-sister relationship is closer than the brother-brother or sister-brother relationship and that this bond, if anything, grows stronger later in life (Cumming and Schneider 1961, p. 499; Adams 1968). In the present study, magazine advertisements reflected the cultural value that all of the above sibling combinations ought to be equally close, although the sister-brother relationship was depicted as slightly closer than the other two. This cultural value did not change significantly since 1920 (Tables C.6 and C.7), except for the sister-brother relationship, where a significant increase was found to have occurred, particularly since 1936 (Figure 6.7). It is possible that as the desired number of children approached two—preferably one of each sex—that the cultural values increasingly supported cross-sexed sibling intimacy.

The studies that have investigated sibling relationships have tended to concentrate on either sibling rivalry or on adult sibling relationships. Because of the "sterilized" viewpoint of family life one gets in advertisements, the present study cannot speak to the issue of sibling rivalry except to say that it is not depicted. Nonetheless, in terms of sibling intimacy throughout the family life cycle, results from the present study indicate that there was no significant change in sister-sister (Table C.8) or brother-sister (Table C.9) intimacy over the parental stages and, if anything, there is a slight but consistent decrease for the sister-sister relationship. Paralleling the research of Cumming and Schneider (1961) and Adams (1968), possibly the sister-sister and brother-sister bond would have been portrayed as closer after adulthood if there had been more advertisements portraying adult sibling interaction. Yet, one must speculate why adult sibling relationships are not emphasized more in magazine advertisements, if they are so important.

Figure 6.8 illustrates that in terms of the brother-brother relationship, a significant decrease in intimacy was found over the parental stages of the family life cycle. Again, the lack of advertisements portraying adult sibling interaction makes it impossible to say much concerning the intimacy between adult brothers. In this case, however, the lack of emphasis is consistent with Adams' (1968) finding that the adult brother-brother relationship is less intimate than the adult

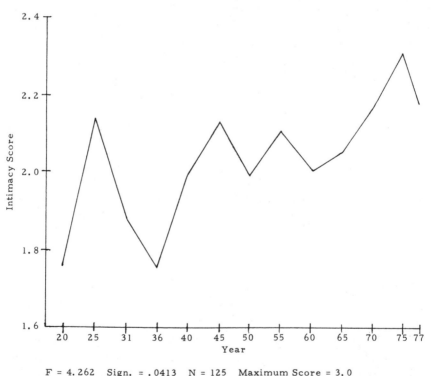

F = 4.262   Sign. = .0413   N = 125   Maximum Score = 3.0

Figure 6.7.   Mean Sister-Brother Intimacy Score by Year.

sister-sister relationship because of males' concern with their occupations and their families of procreation.

Analysis of variance indicated that there were no significant interaction effects between historical time and the family life cycle. An increase in cross-sexed sibling intimacy since 1920 was found for siblings at all stages of the family life cycle (2-way interactions, F = .000, p = 1.00), and the decrease in brother-brother intimacy over the family life cycle was found for all years since 1920 (2-way interactions, F = .018, p = .982). In addition, when siblings were depicted as intimate with each other, they were most likely to be sharing recreational activities. This applied for families at all stages of the family life cycle since 1920.

Overall, an increase in the number of siblings was found to decrease sibling intimacy; sister-sister and brother-brother relationships (Table C.10) showed significant decreases. Taking into account the sex of siblings, increases in the number of female siblings increased

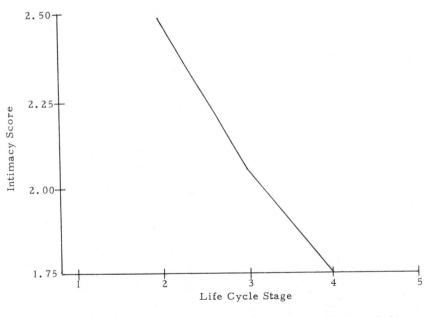

F = 4.442   Sign. = .0419   N = 40   Maximum Score = 3.0

Figure 6.8.   Mean Brother-Brother Intimacy Score by Family Life Cycle.

(although not significantly) sister-sister intimacy (r = .04, p = .410), while increases in the number of male siblings significantly decreased sister-sister intimacy (r = −.39, p = .0170). Similarly, increases in the number of female siblings significantly decreased brother-brother intimacy (r = −.36, p = .0123), whereas increases in the number of male siblings significantly increased brother-brother intimacy (r = .26, p = .0497). Finally, cross-sexed siblings intimacy was found to decrease, although not significantly, as the number of siblings increased, regardless of their sex.

SUMMARY

From 1920 to 1978, intimacy between husbands and wives and between sisters and brothers was found to have increased significantly, at least as depicted in magazine advertising. The portrayal of intimacy between mothers and sons and between fathers and sons, although not changing significantly, did support the shift toward same-sexed family attachments that Martel (1968) found. Contrary to Martel's (1968) findings, mother-daughter intimacy, although increasing between 1920 and 1950, decreased thereafter. Father-daughter intimacy evidenced a cyclical pattern. Finally, sister-sister and brother-brother intimacy was found to have remained fairly constant over the time period covered.

In terms of changes in family intimacy over the family life cycle, a curvilinear relationship was found for husband-wife intimacy, the high points occurring during the preparental and postparental stages. Parent-child intimacy evidenced a decrease during the parental stages. Finally, no significant change in either sister-sister or sister-brother intimacy was noted, although a significant decrease was found in brother-brother intimacy over the family life cycle.

Overall, the evidence from the present chapter supports the contention that intimacy has increased as an important dynamic of family life (see Illustrations 6.1 and 6.2), particularly for certain family relationships at certain stages of the family life cycle and especially with regard to shared recreational activities.

Illustration 6.1.   Medium Degree of Family Intimacy.

(From June 15, 1940 issue of *Life*. Reproduced with permission of Wear-Ever Aluminum Incorporated.)

Illustration 6.2.   High Degree of Family Intimacy.

A growing family has a growing need for financial security.

We have a happy solution.

As your family grows, so do your financial responsibilities.

Our specialty is helping you fulfill them.

With New York Life insurance you can brighten your family's outlook right now and for the years to come.

A well-planned program can build important cash values all the while it protects your wife and children.

It can make your later years brighter by adding to your retirement income.

It can do all this and more.

How many ways can our life insurance enrich your life?

Just ask your New York Life Agent. He'll answer with a smile.

New York Life Insurance Company
51 Madison Avenue, New York, N.Y. 10010
Life, Group and Health Insurance,
Annuities, Pension Plans.
Our 125th year

The "happy life" Company

(From February 6, 1970 issue of *Life*. Reproduced with permission of the New York Life Insurance Company.)

CHAPTER VII

Epilogue

REVIEW OF THE STUDY

The renewed vigor of the feminist movement in the mid-1960s greatly influenced a general concern for and attention to the family unit. Despite varied discussion of "how the family used to be" and "how much the family has changed," scientific investigations have suffered from a basic lack of evidence from an historical perspective. However, it is not only from a lack of historical evidence that the previous research on family roles suffers, but also from a disregard for family role change throughout the family life cycle, as well as an overemphasis on certain family members (in particular, the wife) and aspects of family life (in particular, household chores, child-rearing, and economic provision.) In analyzing images of family life in magazine advertising, it was hoped that some of these deficiencies would be dealt with or eliminated.

Advertising in general interest magazines published between 1920 and 1978 served as the data source. Both the verbal and nonverbal components of the advertisements were used in the analysis. Advertising is considered a good source of historical data on family life values because advertisers, in their efforts to sell a product, try to attract as many potential customers as possible. In order to do so, they must allow as many people as possible to "see themselves" in the advertisement. Also, advertisers have been involved in marketing research since around 1910 and, therefore, have been fairly sophisticated in their analysis and portrayal of basic American values. Finally, certain aspects of family life may be either too personal, too threatening, or simply unknown for more unobtrusive measurement techniques to deal with effectively. However, as Goffman (1976, p. 91) points out, "in advertised worlds we can look in on almost everything."

Each of the dependent variables were measured both qualitatively and quantitatively and were analyzed in terms of historical change since 1920 and family life cycle change. In addition, through the use of two-way analysis of variance, the present study was able to investigate the *separate* effects of historical time while holding family life cycle stage constant, and vice versa. Each of these procedures revealed important information and illustrated what family sociologists have learned—often the hard way—that widely-held assumptions about family life in the past need to be tested.

Briefly, the present analysis found that some values concerning family life have changed more than others, at least as depicted in magazine advertising.[1] The so-called movement toward more egalitarian norms concerning family life has certainly occurred, but the changes have not been undimensional. Values concerning certain aspects of family life were found to change at a different pace than those for other aspects. Some changes were found to have occurred for certain family members, but not for others. Also, some changes were found to be more pronounced for families at particular stages of the family life cycle. Finally, the change that did take place was not necessarily linear. If one assumes that a more egalitarian form of family life involving equal sharing of responsibilities and privileges, along with an increase in companionship and intimacy, is an ideal to strive for, then during certain periods since 1920 our value system, at least as depicted in advertising, has "slipped backwards."

Overall though, the movement toward such an egalitarian ideal in our cultural norms has been fairly substantial, particularly in terms of family companionship and intimacy. The area of family roles still appears to be a major stumbling block. To summarize the findings: the cultural values reflected in magazine advertising increasingly have supported the notion of family members as more companionate and

---

[1] The reader is referred to the individual summaries at the end of Chapters 4 through 6 for a more indepth summary.

intimate (especially in regard to recreation), although they continue to perform their traditional roles almost unchanged.

LIMITATIONS OF THE STUDY

Although one aim of this study was to compensate for some of the weaknesses of previous research, it too has several limitations.

The first limitation is that analysis of magazine advertising gives one a reflection of values concerning the family but not a reflection of family behavior. Cultural norms act as a set of guidelines that usually are flexible enough to permit a fairly wide range of interpretation. Therefore, the present study tells us nothing about how family members actually behaved, although it does tell us what the cultural values were concerning family behavior.

One must also realize that only middle-class cultural values are reflected. All of the general interest magazines analyzed were middle-class publications—this study tells us nothing about the family values of the lower or upper classes.

The remaining limitations are concerned with the measurement techniques. For example, even though the coding scheme was pre-tested and inter-rater reliability was computed, there is always the danger that some unconscious bias may have occurred on the part of the author as the sole coder. Value-free sociology is a myth, but a myth toward which one ought to strive. A team of coders might have had better control over any unconscious bias, thereby rendering the study more value-free.

Another limitation is that the coding of child-care did not make it possible statistically to separate out the "physical care" versus "play" aspects. However, play between parents and children had also been coded under the separate category of recreation, thus making it possible to deal statistically with the play aspects of child-care. When it came to discussing the quantitative changes in the physical care aspects of parenthood, one was left only with child-care scores that combined both the physical care and play aspects. In this case, a qualitative analysis of the data permitted distinction between these two aspects. Since this distinction proved to be so integral, future research should separate these aspects in a quantitative fashion.

The measurement of family intimacy, although theoretically sound, might have been improved by standardizing the measure of distance between family members. This is not to suggest that the subjective evaluation used was grossly invalid. In fact, the coding of distance into three major categories of intimacy undoubtedly compensated for any discrepancies in measurement across advertisements; this was borne out by the high degree of inter-rater reliability. The reason for not using a standardized technique, such as actual measured inches, was not only that different scales were used in individual advertisements, but also because of the problems brought about by having three-dimensional objects on a two-dimensional medium. Because the method used was thought to be more than adequate, such difficulties were avoided in the present study. However, with the increased use and popularity of visual sociology, such methodological issues need to be addressed.

CONTRIBUTIONS OF THE STUDY

In spite of the limitations, the present study has made several contributions. First, in response to the lack of historical and family life cycle data on the aspects of family life analyzed here, the present study serves as a data base of cultural values concerning family life.

Beyond simply serving as a data base, the present study has contributed to the development of sociological theory in terms of the functions Merton (1948) discusses in his classic article.

The serendipity pattern

This "refers to the fairly common experience of observing an unanticipated, anomalous and strategic datum which becomes the occasion for developing a new theory or for extending an existing theory" (Merton 1948, p. 506). In the present study several unanticipated, surprising, and significant results were obtained. For example, the fact that father-daughter intimacy showed such a consistently significant cyclical pattern since 1920 begs for explanation and, therefore, may lead to the development of a new theory. Or, the fact that fathers were portrayed significantly less in child-care activities since 1920 may bring into question the notion that fatherhood has emerged as a more important role for men and, therefore, contribute to the revision of existing theory.

The recasting of theory

Here "it is not that the data are anomalous or unexpected or incompatible with existing theory; it is merely that they have not been considered pertinent" (Merton 1948, p. 509). The inclusion of a family life cycle approach in conjunction with an historical perspective in the present analysis is a contribution to the existing literature and, therefore, may potentially lead to the recasting of theory. For example, it was found that the portrayal of husband-wife intimacy has increased significantly since 1920, but (and here is where the recasting comes in) this was most noticeable for the preparental and postparental stages of the family life cycle.

The refocusing of theoretic interest

"This occurs chiefly through the invention of research procedures which tend to shift the foci of theoretic interest" (Merton 1948, p. 511). In other words, research questions previously "untestable" with existing techniques now become testable. Although neither the use of content analysis nor advertising as a data source is new, it is believed that the present study has contributed to the refocusing of theoretic interest, in particular through the use of the "family intimacy index." The technique used in the present study is seen as a way of extending the potential use of Levinger and Gunner's "interpersonal grid" (1967) to historical materials. For example, now one might be able to analyze the degree of intimacy between family members in even earlier historical periods. Such a technique could be employed on other media where family members have been depicted, such as drawings, paintings, tapestries, etc.

The clarification of concepts

"Empirical research exerts pressure for clear concepts" (Merton 1948, p. 513). The present study has definitely made a contribution to the clarification of concepts. For example, the distinction between companionship and intimacy in the present study, although not entirely resolving the conceptual confusion concerning these terms in family sociology, has at least brought the issue to the fore and, it is hoped, has contributed somewhat to this endeavor.

The "unserendipity" pattern

Although Merton (1948) does not discuss this function of empirical research on the development of sociological theory, it plays an important part. The "unserendipity" pattern refers to results that are anticipated, not surprising, and significant. These types of results contribute to the development of sociological theory either by validating preexisting "common sense knowledge" or by validating previous empirical findings that have played integral parts in existing theory. In other words, by obtaining results consistent with existing theory, one is contributing to the development of sociological theory by increasing our confidence in existing theory. For example, in the present study the fact that children were portrayed almost exlusively in recreational activities increases our confidence in the contention that this has been the century of the child.

THE FUTURE OF FAMILY LIFE VALUES

Earlier in this chapter the point was made that, overall, the movement toward more egalitarian family life values has been fairly substantial since 1920. This was found to be particularly the case in reference to family companionship and family intimacy. But what of the future? What changes in family life values can we expect and possibly even forecast?

Fowles (1976), in his book, *Mass Advertising As Social Forecast*, discusses, describes, and puts to test a method that attempts to forecast social change via advertising. As Fowles (1976, p. 55) describes the rationale underlying his technique:

> The central proposition would be that the fundamental longings of a people prefigure future ways of life and social arrangements.

Fowles (1976) is assuming, as is assumed in the present study, that advertising reflects existing values. However, he goes one step further by asserting that prevailing cultural values—or "needs" as he refers to them—are a prediction of future behavioral changes on a mass scale. There is much validity to Fowles' (1976) argument, and yet, social psychologists have made it abundantly clear that the association between values and behavior is neither strong nor predictable.

Nevertheless, putting this argument aside, of what value can Fowles' (1976) approach be in the present study? It would seem that having a handle on the changes in family life values from 1920 to the present would give one some ability to, at least, suggest likely changes in future family life values. In other words, forecasting future changes in family life values requires less a "leap of faith" than predicting future changes in actual behavior. Indeed, predictions of changes in family life values should be limited to the "near future," say the next ten years or so. It is to this issue that the remainder of the book now turns.

What can we expect family life values to be by the 1990s? Based upon the trend data from the present study, we might expect to see continued deemphasis on housework and child-care for wives. At the same time we may expect increasing emphasis on the sharing of housework by husbands and wives. For husbands, the emphasis on economic provision and child-care will probably show little change. A more likely change will be the increasing emphasis on recreation as an individual and shared activity for all family members.

Little change can be expected in the degree of intimacy between parents and children, with the exception that the cyclical pattern in father-daughter intimacy may well continue. Given a 15-year cycle and a current (1978) low point, one can forecast a shift in values toward increased father-daughter intimacy over the next decade. While same-sexed sibling intimacy will probably not change, the increased intimacy between brothers and sisters can be expected to continue. Husband-wife intimacy will, similarly, evidence a continued increase, particularly for preparental and postparental families.

In conclusion, family life values of the 1990s will emphasize family relationships more intimate than ever before, amid the increased sharing of household tasks by spouses, combined with a heavy emphasis on family fun via shared recreation.

Appendix A

Table A.1.
Frequency and Mean Household Task Score for Wives by
Family Life Cycle*

Life Cycle Stage	Frequency	Mean (max = 1.0)
1	129	.19
2	47	.11
3	45	.13
4	68	.10
5	43	.07
Total	332	.14

*$F = 1.541$ Sign. $= .19$.

Table A.2.
Frequency and Mean Recreation Score for Wives by
Family Life Cycle*

Life Cycle Stage	Frequency	Mean (max = 1.0)
1	129	.50
2	47	.51
3	45	.49
4	68	.68
5	43	.63
Total	332	.55

*$F = 2.002$ Sign. $= .09$.

Table A.3.
Frequency and Percentage of Advertisements Depicting
Wife and Husband Roles in Recreation by the Number
of Children

Number of Children	Wives		Husbands	
	Frequency	Percentage	Frequency	Percentage
0	91	49.7	88	51.2
1	46	25.1	41	23.8
2	36	19.7	36	20.9
3	7	3.8	6	3.5
4	3	1.6	1	.6
Total	183	99.9	172	100.3

Table A.4.
Frequency and Mean Household Task Score for Husbands by Year*

Year	Frequency	Mean (max = 1.0)
1920	22	.05
1925	30	.07
1931	19	.00
1936	20	.00
1940	19	.00
1945	20	.05
1950	28	.07
1955	28	.07
1960	38	.13
1965	36	.03
1970	24	.04
1975	22	.05
1977	26	.00
Total	332	.05

*$F = .933$ Sign. $= .51$.

Table A.5.
Frequency and Mean Household Task Score
for Husbands by Family Life Cycle*

Life Cycle Stage	Frequency	Mean (max = 1.0)
1	129	.05
2	49	.04
3	45	.07
4	66	.06
5	43	.02
Total	332	.05

*$F = .298$ Sign. $= .8792$.

Table A.6.
Frequency and Mean Recreation Score for
Husbands by Family Life Cycle*

Life Cycle Stage	Frequency	Mean (max = 1.0)
1	129	.52
2	49	.45
3	45	.49
4	66	.61
5	43	.49
Total	332	.52

*$F = .818$ Sign. $= .5143$.

Table A.7.
Percentage of Advertisements Depicting Mother and Father Roles in Child-care by the Number of Children

	Number of Children									
	Male			*Female*			*Combined*			
	0	*1*	*2*	*0*	*1*	*2*	*1*	*2*	*3*	*4*
Mother (N=55)	34.5	54.5	10.9	38.2	54.5	7.3	63.6	29.1	5.5	1.8
Father (N=14)	21.4	71.4	7.1	64.3	35.7	0.0	85.7	7.1	7.1	0.0

Table A.8.
Frequency and Percentage of Advertisements Depicting Father-Son and Father-Daughter Companionship in Recreation by Year*

	Father-Son		*Father-Daughter*	
Year	*Frequency*	*Percentage*	*Frequency*	*Percentage*
1920	1	2.50	2	5.00
1925	1	2.04	1	2.04
1931	1	2.56	0	0.00
1936	2	5.13	0	0.00
1940	0	0.00	1	2.94
1945	1	2.56	0	0.00
1950	1	2.22	1	2.22
1955	3	7.14	1	2.38
1960	2	4.00	1	2.00
1965	2	4.44	0	0.00
1970	3	8.11	1	2.70
1975	1	3.57	0	0.00
1977	0	0.00	0	0.00

*N = 521.

Table A.9.
Frequency and Mean Child-care Score for
Fathers by Family Life Cycle*

Life Cycle Stage	Frequency	Mean (max = 1.0)
2	63	.10
3	51	.02
4	86	.08
Total	200	.07

*F = .950 Sign. = .4177.

Table A.10.
Frequency and Mean Recreation Score for
Fathers by Family Life Cycle*

Life Cycle Stage	Frequency	Mean (max = 1.0)
2	63	.37
3	51	.41
4	86	.51
Total	200	.43

*F = 1.394 Sign. = .2460.

Table A.11.
Frequency and Mean Recreation Score for
Brothers by Year*

Year	Frequency	Mean (max = 1.0)
1920	9	.45
1925	11	.82
1931	9	.78
1936	9	.78
1940	8	.88
1945	10	.80
1950	17	.76
1955	14	.86
1960	14	.64
1965	18	.94
1970	9	.89
1975	9	1.00
1977	12	.92
Total	149	.81

*F = 1.435 Sign. = .1571.

Table A.12.
Frequency and Mean Recreation Score for Sons by Year*

Year	Frequency	Mean (max = 1.0)
1920	14	.57
1925	16	.69
1931	17	.65
1936	20	.75
1940	13	.77
1945	17	.82
1950	24	.83
1955	15	.93
1960	26	.69
1965	24	.88
1970	15	.93
1975	14	.79
1977	15	.87
Total	230	.78

*$F = 1.181$ Sign. $= .2977$.

Table A.13.
Frequency and Mean Recreation Score for
Brothers by Family Life Cycle*

Life Cycle Stage	Frequency	Mean (max = 1.0)
2	12	.83
3	90	.81
4	47	.81
Total	149	.81

*$F = .020$ Sign. $= .9806$.

Table A.14.
Frequency and Mean Recreation Score for
Sons by Family Life Cycle*

Life Cycle Stage	Frequency	Mean (max = 1.0)
2	62	.77
3	78	.79
4	85	.80
5	5	.40
Total	230	.78

*F = 1.520 Sign. = .2102.

Table A.15.
Frequency and Mean Recreation Score for Sisters by Year*

Year	Frequency	Mean (max = 1.0)
1920	9	.56
1925	13	.69
1931	8	.88
1936	7	.71
1940	6	.83
1945	11	.64
1950	17	.76
1955	15	.80
1960	13	.62
1965	16	1.00
1970	8	.75
1975	10	1.00
1977	12	.92
Total	145	.79

*F = 1.397 Sign. = .1750.

Table A.16.
Frequency and Mean Recreation Score for
Sisters by Family Life Cycle*

Life Cycle Stage	Frequency	Mean (max = 1.0)
2	10	.90
3	87	.78
4	48	.77
Total	145	.79

*F = .418 Sign. = .6591.

Table A.17.
Frequency and Mean Recreation Score for Daughters
by Year*

Year	Frequency	Mean (max = 1.0)
1920	19	.63
1925	20	.65
1931	17	.76
1936	11	.81
1940	14	.71
1945	19	.57
1950	17	.76
1955	22	.82
1960	19	.68
1965	20	.95
1970	15	.80
1975	10	1.00
1977	15	.93
Total	218	.77

*F = 1.521 Sign. = .1187.

Table A.18.
Frequency and Mean Recreation Score for
Daughters by Family Life Cycle*

Life Cycle Stage	Frequency	Mean (max = 1.0)
2	67	.81
3	75	.79
4	76	.71
Total	218	.77

*F = 1.036 Sign. = .3566.

Appendix B

Table B.1.
Percentage of Advertisements Depicting Husband-Wife Companionship in Household Tasks and Recreation by the Number of Children

| | Number of Children | | | | | | | | | | |
| | Male | | | Female | | | Combined | | | | |
Companionship in	0	1	2	0	1	2	0	1	2	3	4
Household tasks (N = 133)	70.6	11.8	17.6	64.7	17.6	17.6	64.7	5.9	11.8	0.0	17.6
Recreation (N = 418)	97.4	2.6	0.0	96.5	3.5	0.0	95.7	2.6	1.7	0.0	0.0

Table B.2.
Frequency and Mean Husband-Wife Companionship in
Child–care Score by Year*

Year	Frequency	Mean (max = 1.0)
1920	21	.10
1925	16	.00
1931	18	.06
1936	16	.19
1940	12	.08
1945	15	.07
1950	17	.00
1955	13	.00
1960	18	.17
1965	11	.00
1970	10	.30
1975	4	.25
1977	7	.14
Total	178	.09

*$F = 1.363$ Sign. $= .1885$.

Table B.3.
Frequency and Mean Husband-Wife Companionship in
Child–care Score by Family Life Cycle*

Life Cycle Stage	Frequency	Mean (max = 1.0)
2	76	.09
3	49	.02
4	49	.14
5	4	.25
Total	178	.09

*$F = 1.964$ Sign. $= .1212$.

Appendix C

Table C.1.
Frequency and Mean Father–Son Intimacy Score by Year*

Year	Frequency	Mean (max = 3.0)
1920	8	2.3750
1925	7	1.8571
1931	6	2.1667
1936	8	2.1250
1940	7	2.0000
1945	9	2.1111
1950	13	2.0769
1955	11	1.7273
1960	20	1.9000
1965	19	2.2105
1970	13	2.4615
1975	11	2.2727
1977	12	2.0833
Total	144	2.1042

*$F = .342$ Sign. $= .5595$.

Table C.2.
Frequency and Mean Mother–Son Intimacy Score by Year*

Year	Frequency	Mean (max = 3.0)
1920	12	2.2500
1925	13	2.0000
1931	12	1.9167
1936	15	2.4000
1940	10	2.1000
1945	12	2.2500
1950	22	2.0909
1955	14	2.0000
1960	20	2.0500
1965	17	2.0588
1970	11	2.0909
1975	11	2.4545
1977	11	2.1818
Total	180	2.1333

*$F = .067$ Sign. $= .7955$.

Table C.3.
Frequency and Mean Mother-Daughter Intimacy Score
by Year*

Year	Frequency	Mean (max = 3.0)
1920	18	2.3889
1925	21	2.0476
1931	12	1.9167
1936	10	2.1000
1940	10	2.1000
1945	15	2.2000
1950	16	2.3750
1955	20	2.1000
1960	16	2.0625
1965	17	2.1765
1970	12	2.1667
1975	9	1.8889
1977	14	1.9286
Total	190	2.1263

*$F = .937$ Sign. $= .3344$.

Table C.4.
Frequency and Mean Father-Daughter Intimacy Score
by Family Life Cycle*

Life Cycle Stage	Frequency	Mean (max = 3.0)
2	29	2.2759
3	43	1.9302
4	52	1.9808
Total	124	2.0323

*F = 3.146 Sign. = .0786.

Table C.5.
Correlation Between Parent-Child Intimacy and the
Number of Children

Intimacy Relationship	Correlation Coefficient	Significance Level
Mother-Son	−.29	.0000
Father-Son	−.27	.0004
Mother-Daughter	−.15	.0170
Father-Daughter	−.24	.0035

Table C.6.
Frequency and Mean Sister-Sister Intimacy Score by Year*

Year	Frequency	Mean (max = 3.0)
1920	1	2.0000
1925	4	1.7500
1936	3	2.6667
1945	2	1.5000
1950	2	2.5000
1955	3	2.0000
1960	2	1.5000
1965	6	1.5000
1970	4	1.7500
1975	1	1.0000
1977	1	2.0000
Total	29	1.8276

*$F = 1.385$ Sign. $= .2546$.

Table C.7.
Frequency and Mean Brother-Brother Intimacy
Score by Year*

Year	Frequency	Mean (max = 3.0)
1920	3	1.6667
1925	1	2.0000
1931	2	2.0000
1936	5	2.4000
1940	3	2.0000
1945	3	2.3333
1950	1	2.0000
1955	2	2.0000
1960	5	1.6000
1965	7	1.8571
1970	3	2.0000
1975	1	2.0000
1977	4	2.0000
Total	40	1.9750

*$F = .270$ Sign. $= .6075$.

Table C.8.
Frequency and Mean Sister-Sister Intimacy
Score by Family Life Cycle*

Life Cycle Stage	Frequency	Mean (max = 3.0)
2	1	2.0000
3	18	1.8889
4	10	1.7000
Total	29	1.8276

*$F = .419$ Sign. $= .5234$.

Table C.9.
Frequency and Mean Sister-Brother Intimacy Score
by Family Life Cycle*

Life Cycle Stage	Frequency	Mean (max = 3.0)
2	10	2.0000
3	73	2.0822
4	42	2.0238
Total	125	2.0560

*$F = .048$ Sign. $= .8272$.

Table C.10.
Correlation Between Sibling Intimacy and the
Number of Children

Intimacy Relationship	Correlation Coefficient	Significance Level
Sister-Sister	−.39	.0177
Brother-Brother	−.43	.0025
Sister-Brother	−.04	.3482

Bibliography

Adams, Bert N. 1968. *Kinship in an Urban Setting.* Chicago: Markham.
_____. 1970. "Isolation, function, and beyond: American kinship in the 1960's." *Journal of Marriage and the Family* 32 (4):575–97. Also reprinted in C. Broderick, ed. *A Decade Review of Family Research and Action 1960–1969.* Minneapolis, Minn.: National Council on Family Relations, pp. 163–86.

Argyle, Michael. 1975. *Bodily Communication.* New York: International Universities Press.

Aries, Philippe. 1962. *Centuries of Childhood.* Translated by Robert Baldwick. New York: Vintage Books.

Atwell, Saundra Gardner. 1978. "The photo album: Toward a visual analysis of the family." Paper presented at the annual meeting of the American Sociological Association, San Francisco, September.

Baker, Stephen. 1961. *Visual Persuasion: The Effect of Pictures on the Subconscious.* New York: McGraw-Hill.

Ballweg, John A. 1967. "Resolution of conjugal role adjustment after retirement." *Journal of Marriage and the Family* 29 (2):277–81.

Bardwick, Judith M. and Suzanne I. Schumann. 1967. "Portrait of American men and women in TV commercials." *Psychology* 4 (4):18–23.

Bauer, Raymond A. and Stephen A. Greyser. 1968. *Advertising in America: The Consumer View.* Cambridge, Mass.: Harvard University Press.

Berger, Peter L. 1963. *Invitation to Sociology: A Humanistic Perspective.* New York: Doubleday.

Blood, Robert O. and Donald M. Wolfe. 1960. *Husbands and Wives.* New York: The Free Press.

Bose, Christine. 1978. "Technology and changes in the division of labor in the American home." Paper presented at the annual meeting of the American Psychological Association, San Francisco, September.

117

Bridges, W. 1965. "Family patterns and social values in America, 1825–1875." *American Quarterly* 17 (Spring):3–11.

Brown, Bruce W. 1978. "Wife-employment and the emergence of egalitarian marital role prescriptions: 1900–1974." *The Journal of Comparative Family Studies* 9 (1):5–17.

Burgess, Ernest W., Harvey J. Locke, and Mary Margaret Thomes. 1945. *The Family from Institution to Companionship*. New York: American Book.

Burr, Wesley R. 1970. "Satisfaction with various aspects of marriage over the life cycle: a random middle class sample." *Journal of Marriage and the Family* 32 (1):29–37.

Carlson, Rae and Mary Ann Price. 1966. "Generality of social schemas." *Journal of Personality and Social Psychology* 3 (5):589–92.

Chafe, William H. 1972. *The American Woman: Her Changing Social, Economic, and Political Roles, 1920–1970*. New York: Oxford University Press.

Chudacoff, Howard P. and Tamara K. Hareven. 1979. "From the empty nest to family dissolution: Life course transitions into old age." *Journal of Family History* 4 (1):69–83.

Clavan, Sylvia. 1978. "The impact of social class and social trends on the role of grandparent." *The Family Coordinator* 27 (4):351–57.

Courtney, Alice E. and Sarah Wernick Lockeretz. 1971. "A woman's place: An analysis of the roles portrayed by women in magazine advertisements." *Journal of Marketing Research* 8 (1):92–95.

Courtney, Alice E. and Thomas Whipple. 1974. "Women in TV commercials." *Journal of Communications* 24 (2):110–18.

Cumming, Elaine and William Henry. 1961. *Growing Old*. New York: Basic Books.

Cumming, Elaine and David M. Schneider. 1961. "Sibling solidarity: A property of American kinship." *American Anthropologist* 63 (June):498–507.

Curry, Timothy and Alfred C. Clarke. 1977. *Introducing Visual Sociology*. Dubuque, Iowa: Kendall/Hunt.

Demos, John. 1968. "Families in colonial Bristol, R.I." *William and Mary Quarterly* 25 (1):40–57.

———— 1970. *A Little Commonwealth: Family Life in Plymouth Colony*. New York: Oxford University Press.

Demos, John and Virginia Demos. 1969. "Adolescence in historical perspective." *Journal of Marriage and the Family* 31 (4):632–38, as reprinted in M. Gordon, ed. *The American Family in Social-Historical Perspective*. New York: St. Martin's Press, 1973, pp. 209–21.

Dumazedier, Joffre. 1967. *Toward a Sociology of Leisure*. New York: The Free Press.

Easton, Barbara. 1976. "Industrialization and feminity: A case study of nineteenth century New England." *Social Problems* 23 (4):389-402.

Edgell, Stephen. 1972. "Marriage and the concept of companionship." *British Journal of Sociology* 23 (4):452-61.

Edwards, John N. 1967. "The future of the family revisited." *Journal of Marriage and the Family* 29 (3):505-11.

Elder, Glen H. 1977. "Family history and the life course." *Journal of Family History* 2 (4):279-304.

Filene, Peter G. 1974. *Him, Her, Self: Sex Roles in Modern America.* New York: New American Library.

Fogel, R. 1975. "Limits of quantitative methods in history." *American Historical Review* 80 (2):329-50.

Fowles, Jib. 1976. *Mass Advertising as Social Forecast: A Method for Futures Research.* Westport, Conn.: Greenwood.

Furstenberg, Frank. 1966. "Industrialization and the American family: A look backward." *American Sociological Review* 31 (3):326-37, as reprinted in M.B. Sussman, ed. *Sourcebook in Marriage and the Family.* Boston: Houghton Mifflin, 1974, pp. 30-40.

Gaw, Walter A. 1961. *Advertising: Methods and Media.* San Francisco: Wadsworth.

Gillmor, Donald M. and Jerome A. Barron. 1969. *Mass Communication Law.* St. Paul, Minn.: West.

Glick, Paul C. 1977. "Updating the life cycle of the family." *Journal of Marriage and the Family* 39 (1):5-13.

Goffman, Erving. 1976. "Gender advertisements." *Studies in the Anthropology of Visual Communication* 3 (2):69-154.

Gordon, Michael. 1969. "The ideal husband as depicted in the 19th century marriage manual." *The Family Coordinator* 18 (3):226-30.

Gordon, Michael and M. Charles Bernstein. 1970. "Mate choice and domestic life in the 19th century marriage manual." *Journal of Marriage and the Family* 32 (4):665-73.

Gordon, Michael and Tamara Hareven. 1973. "New social history of the family." *Journal of Marriage and the Family* 35 (3):393-495.

Hall, E.T. 1959. *The Silent Language.* New York: Doubleday.

Hareven, Tamara K. 1976. "The last stage: Historical adulthood and old age." *Daedalus* 105 (4):13-28.

———— 1977a. "Family time and historical time." *Daedalus* 106 (2):57-70.

———— 1977b. "The family life cycle in historical perspective: A proposal for a developmental approach." In *Le cycle de la vie familiale dans les societes europeenes,* edited by J. Cuisenier and M. Segalen, pp. 339-52. The Hague: Mouton.

Hepner, Harry Walker. 1941. *Effective Advertising.* New York: McGraw-Hill.

Hobart, Charles W. 1963. "Commitment, value conflict, and the future of the family." *Marriage and Family Living* 25 (2):405-12.

Holder, Stephen C. 1973. "The family magazine and the American people." *Journal of Popular Culture* 7 (2):264-79.

Irish, Donald P. 1964. "Sibling interaction: A neglected aspect in family life research." *Social Forces* 42:279-88.

Kelly, John R. 1972. "The family and leisure: Finding a function." Paper presented at the annual meeting of the National Council on Family Relations, Portland, Oregon.

Kerckhoff, Alan C. 1964. "Husband-wife expectations and reactions to retirement." *Journal of Gerontology* 19 (4):510-16.

————. 1972. "The structure of the conjugal relationship in industrial society." In *Cross-National Family Research*, edited by M.B. Sussman and B.E. Cogswell, pp. 53-69. Leiden, Netherlands: E.J. Brill.

Kilbourne, Jean. 1977. "Images of women in TV commercials." In *TV Book*, edited by Judy Fireman, pp. 293-96. New York: Workman.

Kirkpatrick, Clifford. 1936. "A comparison of generations in regard to attitudes toward feminism." *Journal of Genetic Psychology* 49 (December):343-61.

Komisar, Lucy. 1972. "The image of women in advertising." In *Women in Sexist Society*, edited by V. Gornick and B.K. Moran, pp. 207-17. New York: New American Library.

Labovitz, Sanford. 1968. "Criteria for selecting a significance level: A note on the sacredness of .05." *American Sociologist* 3 (August):220-22.

————. 1972. "Statistical usage in sociology: Sacred cows and ritual." *Sociolocical Methods and Research* 1 (1):13-37.

Lantz, Herman R., E.C. Snyder, M. Britton, and R. Schmitt. 1968. "Pre-industrial patterns in the colonial family in America: A content analysis of colonial magazines." *American Sociological Review* 33 (3):413-26.

Lantz, Herman R., Raymond L. Schmitt, and Richard Herman. 1973. "The pre-industrial family in America: A further examination of early magazines." *American Journal of Sociology* 79 (3):566-88.

Lantz, Herman R., J. Keyes, and Martin Schultz. 1975. "The family in the pre-industrial period: From base lines in history to change." *American Sociological Review* 40 (1):21-36.

Lantz, Herman R., Martin Schultz, and Mary O'Hara. 1977. "The changing American family from the pre-industrial to the industrial period: A final report." *American Sociological Review* 42 (3):406-21.

Lazarsfeld, Paul F. and Robert K. Merton. 1957. "Mass communication, popular taste, and organized social action." In *Mass Culture*, edited by Bernard Rosenberg and David Manning White. Glencoe, Ill.: Free Press.

Levinger, G. 1964. "Task and social behavior in marriage." *Sociometry* 27 (4):433-48.

Levinger G. and J. Gunner. 1967. "The interpersonal grid: Felt and tape techniques for the measurement of social relationships." *Psychonomic Science* 8 (4):173-74.

Leymore, Varda Langholz. 1975. *Hidden Myth: Structure and Symbolism in Advertising.* New York: Basic Books.

Lipman, Aaron. 1961. "Role conceptions and morale of couples in retirement." *Journal of Gerontology* 16:267-71.

Little, K.B. 1965. "Personal space." *Journal of Experimental Social Psychology* 1 (3):237-47.

Lopata, Helena Znaniecki. 1966. "The life cycle of the social role of the housewife." *Sociology and Social Research* 51 (October):5-22.

Lott, D.F. and R. Sommer. 1967. "Seating arrangements and status." *Journal of Personality and Social Psychology* 7 (1):90-95.

Lyons, Bill. 1969. "Do ad men live by obvious myths?" *Marketing/Communications* 297 (March), as reprinted in J.S. Wright and J.E. Mertes, eds. *Advertising's Role in Society.* New York: West, 1974, pp. 13-17.

Macionis, John J. 1978. "Intimacy: Structure and process in interpersonal relationships." *Alternatives: Marriage, Family and Changing Lifestyles* 1 (1): 113-30.

Martel, Martin. 1968. "Age-sex roles in American magazine fiction 1890-1955." In *Middle Age and Aging,* edited by B. Neugarten, pp. 47-57. Chicago: University of Chicago Press.

Mason, Karen Oppenheim, John L. Czajka, and Sara Arber. 1976. "Change in women's sex-role attitudes, 1964-1974." *American Sociological Review* 41 (4):573-96.

Maxwell, Joseph W. 1976. "The keeping fathers of America." *The Family Coordinator* 25 (4):387-92.

Mayer, L.S. 1971. "A note on treating ordinal data as interval data." *American Sociological Review* 36 (3):519-20.

McGovern, James R. 1968. "The American women's pre-World War I freedom in manners and morals." *Journal of American History* 55 (2):315-33.

McLuhan, Marshall. 1964. "Ads: Keeping upset with the Joneses." From *Understanding Media: The Extensions of Man.* New York: McGraw-Hill, 1971, as reprinted in J.S. Wright and J.E. Mertes, eds. *Advertising's Role in Society.* New York: West, 1974, pp. 5-9.

_____. 1971. *Understanding Media.* New York: McGraw-Hill.

Medley, Morris L. 1977. "Marital adjustment in the post-retirement years." *The Family Coordinator* 26 (1):5-11.

Mehrabian, A. 1969. "Significance of posture and position in the communication of attitude and status relationships." *Psychological Bulletin* 71 (5):359-72.

Merton, Robert K. 1948. "The bearing of empirical research upon the development of social theory." *American Sociological Review* 13 (5):505-15.

Miller, Brent C. 1975. "Studying the quality of marriage cross-sectionally." *Journal of Marriage and the Family* 37 (2):11–12.

Millum, Trevor. 1975. *Images of Women.* Totowa, N.J.: Bowman and Littlefield.

Morgan, W.L. and A.M. Leahy. 1934. "The cultural content of general interest magazines." *Journal of Educational Psychology* 25 (October):530–36.

Neugarten, Bernice L. and Karol K. Weinstein. 1964. "The changing American grandparent." *Journal of Marriage and the Family* 26 (1):199–204.

Nimkoff, M.F. 1961. "Changing family relationships of older people in the United States during the last fifty years." *The Gerontologist* 1 (1):91–99.

Nye, F. Ivan. 1976. *Role Structure and Analysis of the Family.* Beverly Hills, Calif.: Sage.

Orthner, Dennis K. 1975. "Leisure activity patterns and marital satisfaction over the marital career." *Journal of Marriage and the Family* 37 (1):91–102.

Osmond, Marie Withers and Patricia Yancey Martin. 1975. "Sex and sexism: A comparison of male and female sex-role attitudes." *Journal of Marriage and the Family* 37 (4):744–59.

Parelius, Ann P. 1975. "Emerging sex-role attitudes, expectations, and strains among college women." *Journal of Marriage and the Family* 37 (1):146–53.

Parke, Ross D. and Douglas B. Sawin. 1977. "The father's role in infancy: A re-evaluation." *The Family Coordinator* 25 (4):365–71.

Parsons, Talcott and R.F. Bales. 1955. *Family Socialization and Interaction Process.* New York: The Free Press.

Peterson, Theodore. 1964. *Magazines in the Twentieth Century.* Urbana: University of Illinois Press.

Powell, Kathryn S. 1963. "Family variables." In *The Employed Mother in America,* edited by F.I. Nye and L.W. Hoffman, pp. 231–40. Chicago: Rand McNally.

Raina, M.K. 1975. "Parental perception about ideal child: A cross-cultural study." *Journal of Marriage and the Family* 37 (1):229–32.

Rendina, Irma and Jean D. Dickerscheid. 1977. "Father involvement with first-born infants." *The Family Coordinator* 25 (4):373–78.

Robertson, Joan F. 1976. "Significance of grandparents: Perceptions of young adult grandchildren." *The Gerontologist* 16 (1):137–40.

_____. 1977. "Grandmotherhood: A study of role conceptions." *Journal of Marriage and the Family* 39 (1):165–74.

Rollins, Boyd C. and Kenneth L. Cannon. 1974. "Marital satisfaction over the family life cycle: A reevaluation." *Journal of Marriage and the Family* 36 (2):271–82.

Rollins, Mabel A. 1963. "Monetary contributions of wives to family income in 1920 and 1960." *Marriage and Family Living* 25 (2):226–27.

Roper, Brent S. and Emily LaBeff. 1977. "Sex roles and feminism revisited: An intergenerational attitude comparison." *Journal of Marriage and the Family* 39 (1):113–19.

Rosenblatt, Paul C. 1974. "Behavior in public places: Comparison of couples accompanied and unaccompanied by children." *Journal of Marriage and the Family* 36 (4):750–55.

Rutman, Darrett B. 1973. "Notes to the underground: Historiography." *Journal of Interdisciplinary History* 3 (2):373–83.

Safilios-Rothschild, Constantina. 1970. "The study of family power: A review 1960–1969." *Journal of Marriage and the Family* 32 (4):539–49.

————. 1972. "Instead of a discussion: Companionate marriages and sexual equality: Are they compatible?" In *Toward a Sociology of Women*, edited by C. Safilios-Rothschild, pp. 63–70. Lexington, Mass.: Xerox College.

Scanzoni, Letha and John Scanzoni. 1976. *Men, Women, and Change: A Sociology of Marriage and the Family*. New York: McGraw-Hill.

Schlesinger, Arthur, Jr. 1962. "The humanist looks at empirical social research." *American Sociological Review* 27 (6):768–71.

Schneider, Kenneth R. 1968. "Will of advertising." From *Destiny of Change: How Relevant is Man in the Age of Development*. New York: Holt, Rinehart and Winston, as reprinted in J.S. Wright and J.E. Mertes, eds. *Advertising's Role in Society*. New York: West, 1974, pp. 106–10.

Schram, Rosalyn Weinman. 1979. "Marital satisfaction over the family life cycle: A critique and proposal." *Journal of Marriage and the Family* 41 (1):7–12.

Shorter, Edward. 1975. *The Making of the Modern Family*. New York: Basic Books.

Slater, P.E. 1961. "Parental role differentiation." *American Journal of Sociology* 67 (3):296–308.

Smith, Daniel Scott. 1973. "Parental power and marriage patterns: An analysis of historical trends in Hingham, Massachusetts." *Journal of Marriage and the Family* 35 (3):419–28.

Sommer, R. 1961. "Leadership and group geography." *Sociometry* 24 (1):99–110.

————. 1967. "Small group ecology." *Psychological Bulletin* 67 (1):145–51.

Spanier, Graham B., Robert A. Lewis, and Charles L. Cole. 1975. "Marital adjustment over the family life cycle: The issue of curvilinearity." *Journal of Marriage and the Family* 37 (2):263–75.

Stinnett, Nick, Linda Mittelstet Carter, and James E. Montgomery. 1972. "Older persons' perceptions of their marriages." *Journal of Marriage and the Family* 34 (4):665–70.

Stone, Carol. 1963. "Family recreation, a parental dilemma." *The Family Coordinator* 12 (1):85–87.

Straus, Murray A. and Bruce W. Brown. 1978. *Family Measurement Techniques*. Revised Edition. Minneapolis: University of Minnesota Press.

Titus, Sandra L. 1976. "Family photographs and transition to parenthood." *Journal of Marriage and the Family* 38 (3):525–30.

Updegroff, Robert R. 1972. *The Power of the Obvious*. Littleton, N.H.: Executive Press.

Venkatesan, M. and Jean Losco. 1975. "Women in magazine ads: 1959–1971." *Journal of Advertising Research* 15 (5):49–54.

Wagner, L. and J. Banos. 1973. "Women's place: A follow-up." *Journal of Marketing Research* 10 (May):213–14.

Waite, Linda J. 1976. "Working wives: 1940–1960." *American Sociological Review* 41 (1):65–79.

Wald, Carol. 1975. *Myth America: Picturing Women, 1865-1945.* New York: Pantheon.

_____. 1977. "U.S. male." *Print* 31 (November/December): 56–61.

Ward, Russell A. 1978. "Limitations of the family as a supportive institution in the lives of the aged." *The Family Coordinator* 27 (4):365–73.

Webb, Eugene J., Donald T. Campbell, Richard D. Schwartz, and Lee Sechrest. 1966. *Unobtrusive Measures: Nonreactive Research in the Social Sciences.* Chicago: Rand McNally.

Weitzman, Lenore J. 1975. "To love, honor and obey? Traditional legal marriage and alternative family forms." *The Family Coordinator* 24 (4):531–48.

Welter, Barbara. 1966. "The cult of true womanhood: 1820–1860." *American Quarterly* 18 (2):151–74, as reprinted in M. Gordon, ed. *The American Family in Social-Historical Perspective.* New York: St. Martin's Press, 1973, pp. 224–50.

Wolfenstein, Martha. 1952. "The emergence of fun morality." *Journal of Social Issues* 7 (4):10–15, as reprinted in J.P. Spradley and M.A. Rynkiewich, eds. *The Nacirema.* Boston: Little, Brown, 1975.

Women on Words and Images. 1975. "The medium is macho." *Human Behavior* 4 (August):71.

Wood, James Playsted. 1956. *Magazines in the United States.* 2nd ed. New York: The Ronald Press.

Wright, John S. and John E. Mertes, eds. 1974. *Advertising's Role in Society.* New York: West.

Index

Adams, B.N., 7, 51, 65, 81, 83, 84
Adolescents, 22, 39, 59; (*see also* children)
Advertisements: 3; basic premise of, 11;
   brand name, 10; coding of, 20–25; creat-
   ing desires through, 12; criteria for selecting, 17; data source of, 15–17, 89;
   empirical evidence for reflecting cultural
   values in, 13; ethics in, 11; frequency of,
   by magazine, 20; frequency of, by year
   and family life cycle stage, 19, 20, 21;
   individual vs. mass values in, 12; inter-
   rater reliability of, 18, 21; law concerning, 16–17; magazine, 4, 5, 9–14; men's
   images in, 1, 4, 7; page position of, 10;
   reinforcing cultural values in, 13; sampling procedures for study of, 17–19;
   shaping vs. reflecting cultural values in,
   11–14, 15, 94; size of, 10; truth in, 11,
   16; unambiguous nature of, 18; unobtrusive nature of, 15, 16, 90; women's
   image in, 3, 4, 5, 13, 14
Affection, 4, 6, 73
American, 18, 20
Arber, S., 2, 3
Argyle, M., 24
Aries, P., 49
Atwell, S.G., 15
Authority: family, 5; grandparents, 52

Baby boom: husband-wife intimacy during,
   76; mother-father companionship in
   child-care during, 58, 59; mothers'
   responsibility for child-care during, 43
Baker, S., 12
Bales, R.F., 64

Ballweg, J.A., 39
Banos, J., 14
Bardwick, J.M., 4, 7
Barron, J.A., 16
Bauer, R.A., 13
Bernstein, M.C., 2
Blood, R.O., 5, 59
Bonds: father-son, 6; mother-child, 31;
   mother-daughter, 6
Bose, C., 32
Brand names: use of, in advertising, 10
Bridges, W., 2
Britton, M., 2, 5
Brothers: 1; housework by, 50; intimacy of,
   with other siblings, 83–86; recreation by,
   49, 50, 54, 66–67; (*see also* siblings)
Brown, A., 9
Brown, B.W., 5, 73
Burgess, E. W., 73, 77
Burr, W.R., 61

Campbell, D.T., 16
Cannon, K.L., 62
Careers (*see* employment)
Carlson, R., 24
Carter, L.M., 77
Chafe, W.H., 17
Child-care: 23, 24; family role changes and,
   7; fathers' role in, 26, 46–49; fathers' responsibility for play vs. physical care
   aspects of, 46–49, 53, 58; "fun morality"
   in, 43; future of, 95; husband-wife intimacy and, 76; limitations in coding of,
   91; mother-father companionship in,
   58, 59, 68; mothers' responsibility for,

125

About the Author

BRUCE W. BROWN is Assistant Professor of Sociology at Wilkes College in Wilkes-Barre, Pennsylvania. He holds a B.A. from the State University of New York at Plattsburgh and a M.A. and Ph.D. from the University of New Hampshire.

Dr. Brown has published articles in *The Family Coordinator, The Journal of Comparative Family Studies, Sex Roles: A Journal of Research,* and *The Social Causes of Husband-Wife Violence* (edited by M.A. Straus and G. T. Hotaling). He is coauthor, with M.A. Straus, of *Family Measurement Techniques* (University of Minnesota Press, 1978) and editor of *Readings in Family Sociology* (Ginn, 1980).